Town Maps

1st Edition

Town	Page No.
Ashbourne	56 - 57
Athboy	31
Balbriggan	42 - 43
Bettystown	26 - 27
Blessington	80 - 81
Clane	72 - 73
Delgany	84 - 85
Donabate	60 - 61
Drogheda	17 - 25
Duleek	38 - 39
Dundalk	3 - 15
Dunshaughlin	52 - 53
Greystones	82 - 83
Kells	30
Kilcock	68 - 69
Laytown	28 - 29
Lusk	48 - 49
Naas	74 - 79
Naul	41
Navan	32 - 37
Portraine	58 - 59
Prosperous	70
Ratoath	54 - 55
Rush	50 - 51
Sallins	71
Skerries	44 - 45
Slane	16
Stamullin	40
Swords	62 - 67
Trim	46 - 47

Compiled and published by Ordnance Survey Ireland,
Phoenix Park, Dublin 8, Ireland.

Arna thiomsú agus arna fhoilsiú ag Suirbhéireacht Ordanáis Éireann,
Páirc an Fhionnuisce, Baile Átha Cliath 8, Éire.

All Town Maps are produced from Osi Largescale revisions from 2004/5 with local infills.
Historic Map extracts taken from the Ordnance Survey Ireland Historic Map Archive.
www.irishhistoricmaps.ie

Printed by the Print Consortium of Ireland.

Paper used to produce this publication is biodegradeable
and comes from replanted forests in Europe and North America.

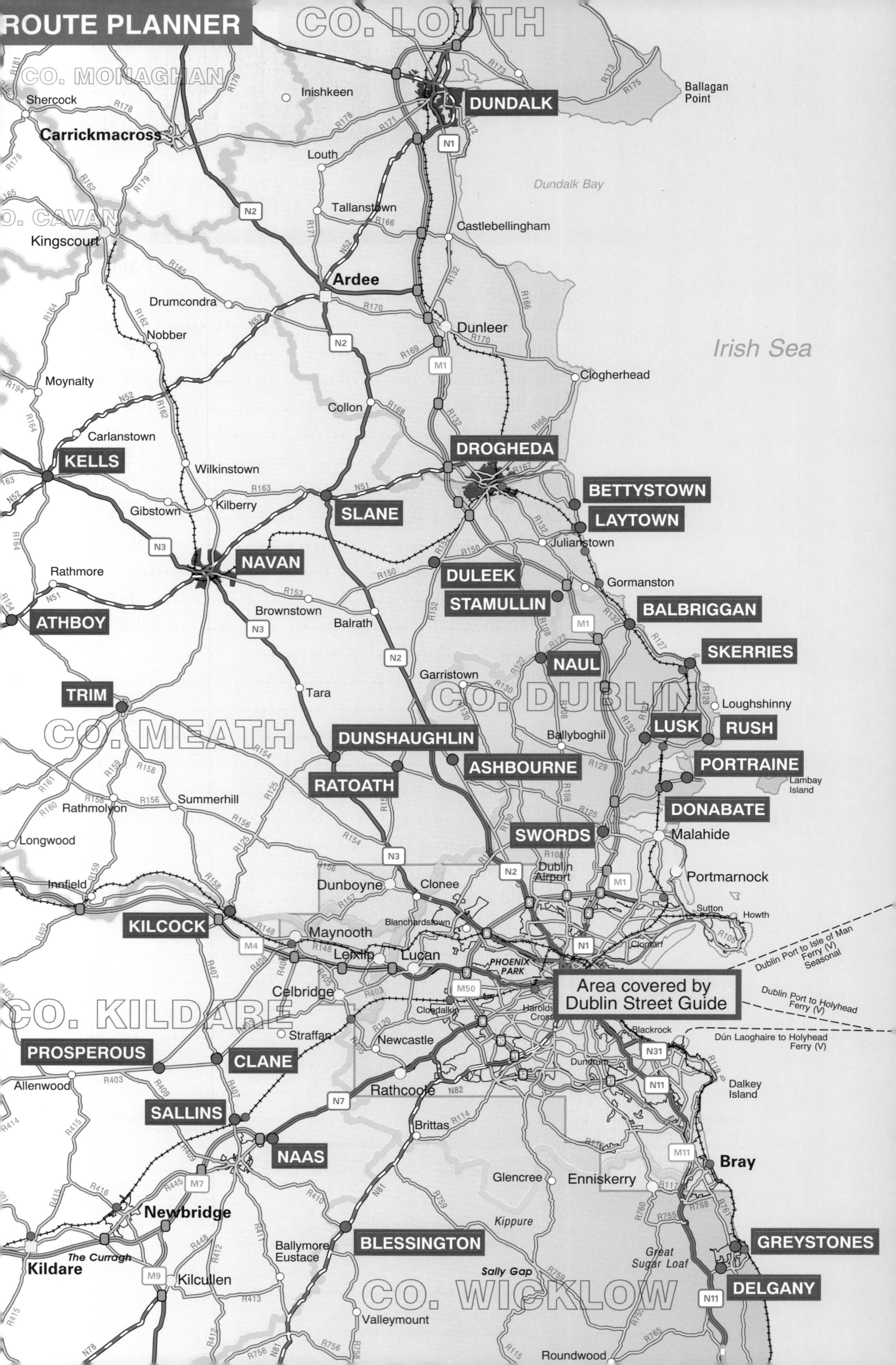
ROUTE PLANNER
CO. LOUTH
CO. MONAGHAN
CO. CAVAN
CO. MEATH
CO. DUBLIN
CO. KILDARE
CO. WICKLOW
Irish Sea
Dundalk Bay
DUNDALK
Ballagan Point
Inishkeen
Shercock
Carrickmacross
Louth
Tallanstown
Kingscourt
Castlebellingham
Ardee
Drumcondra
Dunleer
Nobber
Clogherhead
Moynalty
Collon
Carlanstown
KELLS
DROGHEDA
Wilkinstown
BETTYSTOWN
Gibstown
Kilberry
SLANE
LAYTOWN
Julianstown
NAVAN
DULEEK
Rathmore
Gormanston
STAMULLIN
Brownstown
ATHBOY
Balrath
BALBRIGGAN
SKERRIES
NAUL
Garristown
TRIM
Tara
Loughshinny
LUSK
RUSH
Ballyboghil
DUNSHAUGHLIN
ASHBOURNE
PORTRAINE
RATOATH
Lambay Island
DONABATE
Summerhill
Rathmolyon
Longwood
SWORDS
Malahide
Dublin Airport
Portmarnock
Dunboyne
Clonee
Innfield
Sutton
Howth
KILCOCK
Blanchardstown
Maynooth
Clontarf
Leixlip
Lucan
PHOENIX PARK
Dublin Port to Isle of Man Ferry (V) Seasonal
Area covered by Dublin Street Guide
Celbridge
Clondalkin
Harolds Cross
Dublin Port to Holyhead Ferry (V)
Blackrock
Straffan
Newcastle
Dún Laoghaire to Holyhead Ferry (V)
PROSPEROUS
CLANE
Dundrum
Allenwood
Rathcoole
Dalkey Island
SALLINS
Brittas
NAAS
Bray
Glencree
Enniskerry
Newbridge
Kippure
BLESSINGTON
GREYSTONES
The Curragh
Ballymore Eustace
Great Sugar Loaf
Kildare
Sally Gap
Kilcullen
DELGANY
Valleymount
Roundwood

INDEX

ton Drive E5
hameen Park F6
dans Close C3
sling Park C3
bert Place D4
naverna Drive C5
ne Street D5
d Easmuin Road D4
d Na Mara F9
d Shee F9
dee Lane C5
dee Road C5
dee Road D5
dee Road Bridge D5
dee Terrace C5
cal Emer G9
cal Setanta F9
hbrook E5
hbrook Avenue E5
hdale Park F5
hford Crescent E6
hgrove F5
sumption Place D3
lt Bridge B3
enue Park E5
enue Road E5
enue Road F5
ondale Park E5
chelors Walk D4
rleyfield C1
rrack Close F4
rrack Mews E4
rrack Street E4
rton Park C3
ech Park G9
echmount Drive C4
echmount Park C4
lfry Crescent E5
lfry Drive E5
lfry Gardens E5
llews Bridge Road C2
llfield View E9
rches Lane G8
shop Court E4
ackrock Cove G8
ackrock Road F6
ackrock Road G7
ackwater Court E5
akely Close E5
thair Blinne C4
thar Brú C4
thar Maol F7
yle O'Reilly Terrace D3
ckfield Close D3
dge Street D3
dge Water Mews D4
ook Street C5
ookfield D8
ookwood Lawns F5
oughton Street E4
own's Quay E4
ttercrane Lane E4
rraig Ard F9
rrickmacross Road C5
rrickmacross Rd Bridge D5
rroll Mead D4
stle Heights C3
stle Park C3
stle Road E4
stleross C3
stletown Cross Rds C3
stletown Road B3
stletown Road Bridge D3
darwood Park C4
apel Pass G8
apel Road E8
apel Street D4
erry Vale F5
estnut Grove F5
urch Park G8
urch Street D4
addagh Park E5
anbrassil Street D4
ann Chullain C4
ermont Bridge C9
ermont Estate E9
ermont Park E9
oneen Drive C4
ontygora Court F6
ós Deirdrú G9
uain Enda E5
burn Road F5
ckle Hill F9
bes Road F4
bis Aodhan C3
bis Brid C3
bis Cormac C3
bis Croinn C3
llege Court D4
llege Heights E6
nnick's Quay E4
oley Park F4
ttage Lane F9
owe Street D4
umlin Bridge D7
uchullain Terrace D3
ulhane Street D4
ypress Gardens F5
e La Salla Terrace D3
eerpark B5
efenders Row D4
emense Road D4
emesne Terrace D5
stillery Lane E4
oolargy F6
oolargy Avenue F6

Doylesfort Grove E2
Doylesfort Road D2
Dublin Road D5
Dublin Street D5
Dún Mhic Cainte C4
Dundalk Junction D5
Dunmore D5
Earl Street D4
Eastern By-Pass Road F7
Elm Grove F5
Elm Park G8
Emer Terrace D3
Fairgreen Road D3
Fairgreen Row D4
Fairview G8
Famdreg Close C4
Famdreg Estate C4
Father Murray Park D3
Fatima Court C3
Fatima Drive C3
Fatima Park C3
Faughart Terrace E4
Ferns Cove G9
Fernwood F5
Forkhill Road D3
Francis Street D4
Garrybawn E5
George's Street E4
Glenmore Park F6
Glenwood Close E6
Glenwood Estate E6
Gort Na Glaise F8
Gosling's Terrace D5
Grange Close F6
Grange Drive F6
Green Acres E5
Greenfield Court E5
Greenwood Drive F5
Griffith Court D4
Hamilton Drive F8
Haynestown Bridge D8
Hazel Court F5
Hazelwood Avenue F5
Hazelwood Court F5
Headford Estate C3
Hill Street D5
Hill Street Bridge D5
Hill View D4
Hill's Lane D5
Hoey's Lane E6
Holly Park F5
Hughes Park D5
Hyde Park F4
Jocelyn Court E4
Jocelyn Drive E4
Jocelyn Street E4
John Street D4
Keleo Terrace E4
Kincora Terrace D5
Kingswood F6
Knockbridge Road B6
Lady Well Terrace D5
Langfield D6
Laurel Brook Close D4
Laurel Brook Gardens D4
Laurel Grove E5
Laurels Road D4
Legion Avenue D4
Lennon-Melia Terrace D3
Lennonstown Avenue F4
Lennonstown Close F4
Lennonstown Crescent F4
Lennonstown Green F4
Lennonstown Manor F4
Line Terrace D5
Linenhall Street D4
Lisnaree E5
Lower Point Road H4
Mac Swiney Street D4
Magnet Road D4
Main Street G8
Manydown Close F4
Maple Close F5
Marian Park C3
Marine Avenue G8
Marine Court G8
Marine Crescent G8
Marine Drive G8
Marine View G8
Market Square D4
Market Street D4
Marlbog Road D9
Mary Street D5
Mary Street North E4
Maxwell's Cottages D3
Maxwell's Row D3
Maxwell's Terrace D3
Mayfield Drive E9
McDermott's Terrace C5
McEntee Avenue D4
Meadow Grove Estate E4
Meadow View F5
Medebawn F5
Meeting House Lane D3
Mill Road B3
Mill Street E4
Moira Terrace D3
Moorland Road D3
Mount Avenue C4
Mountain Court F4
Mountain View F4
Mountain View Crescent F4
Mountain View Terrace E4
Mounthamilton C5
Mounthamilton Close C5
Mourne Vale E5

Mourne View D5
Muirhevna E6
Muirhevnamore F5
Mulholland Avenue D4
Mullagharlin Road D8
Mullaharlin Road E7
Naughton's Close E6
New Golf Links Lane G8
New Quay E4
New Street E4
Newry Road E2
Nicholas Street D4
Northgate Street D3
Oakes Quay E4
Oakland Park C4
Oaklawns E5
Oakvale Park F5
O'Hanlon Park East D4
O'Hanlon Park West D4
O'Hanlon Street North D4
O'Hanlon Street South D4
Old Golf Links Road F8
Oldbridge Estate C2
Oliver Plunkett Park D4
Park Avenue D4
Park Drive D4
Park Street D4
Park View D4
Park Villas D4
Parnell Park D5
Patrick Street D4
Pearse Park D4
Peter Street F4
Philip Street D4
Pinewood Grove F5
Point Road F4
Priorland Gardens D6
Priorland Grove D6
Priorland Road D6
Priory Villas D4
Quay Street E4
Racecourse Road E3
Railway Quay E4
Railway Terrace D5
Rampart Lane D4
Rampart Road E4
Rampart Road D5
Rath Conaille C4
Rath Park C6
Rathmount Estate F9
Red Barns Road F5
Regan's Terrace D5
Riverside Crescent D3
River Lane D4
Riverside Drive G4
Riverwell Close C2
Rock Court F9
Rock Road G8
Rock Ville F8
Rockfield Court E6
Rockfield Manor E6
Rockmount G8
Rockmount Gardens C5
Roden Place E4
Rosewood F5
Ruinn Colmcille D4
Saltown C3
Sandfield Gardens G8
Sandy Grove F8
Sandy Grove Close F8
Sandy Lane G9
Sandymount G8
Sandymount Drive G8
Seacrest Manor H4
Seafield Gardens G9
Seafield Lawns E5
Seafield Road F9
Seatown E4
Seatown Gardens E4
Seatown Place E4
Seaview Terrace E3
Shore Road G5
Sliabh Foy Park F6
South End G9
Springfield F9
Springfield Manor F5
St Alphonsus Road E4
St Alphonsus Close E5
St Alphonsus Road E5
St Anne's Court D5
St Brigid's Terrace E4
St Clement's Park F4
St Domnick's Place D5
St Fursey's Terrace F9
St Gerard's Square E4
St Helena Terrace E4
St Johns Court D4
St Joseph's Park E4
St Kevin's Terrace E3
St Leonard's Garden E4
St Malachy's Villas D5
St Mary's Court E4
St Mary's Road E4
St Nicholas Avenue D3
St Nicholas Gardens D3
St Patrick's Terrace E4
St Ronan's Terrace C3
Stapelton Place D5
Stapleton Drive D5
Suil Na Mara G4
Sutton Court E4
The Arches D4
The Crescent D5
The Demense D4
The Ferns G9
The Links F8

The Loakers F7
The Long Avenue D5
The Long Walk D4
The Meadows (off Point Rd) F4
The Meadows (off Rock Rd) G8
The Orchard G8
The Rock Road F8
The Square G8
Thomas Street D5
Thomastown Bridge A6
Toberona Cottages B2
Tom Bellew Avenue E5
Tuite's Lane F8
Union Street D4
Villa Park E5
Village Green G7
Vincent Avenue D5
Wallace Cove F9
Water View H4
Waterville Crescent E5
Wavecrest Drive G9
Wellington Place D4
Williamson's Place D4
Willow Dale F5
Willow Grove C5
Windmill Court E4
Wolfe Tone Terrace D4
Woodbury Gardens E5
Woodland Drive C5
Woodview Park D3
Woodview Terrace D3
Woodville Manor E6
Wynne's Terrace D5
Yorke Street D4

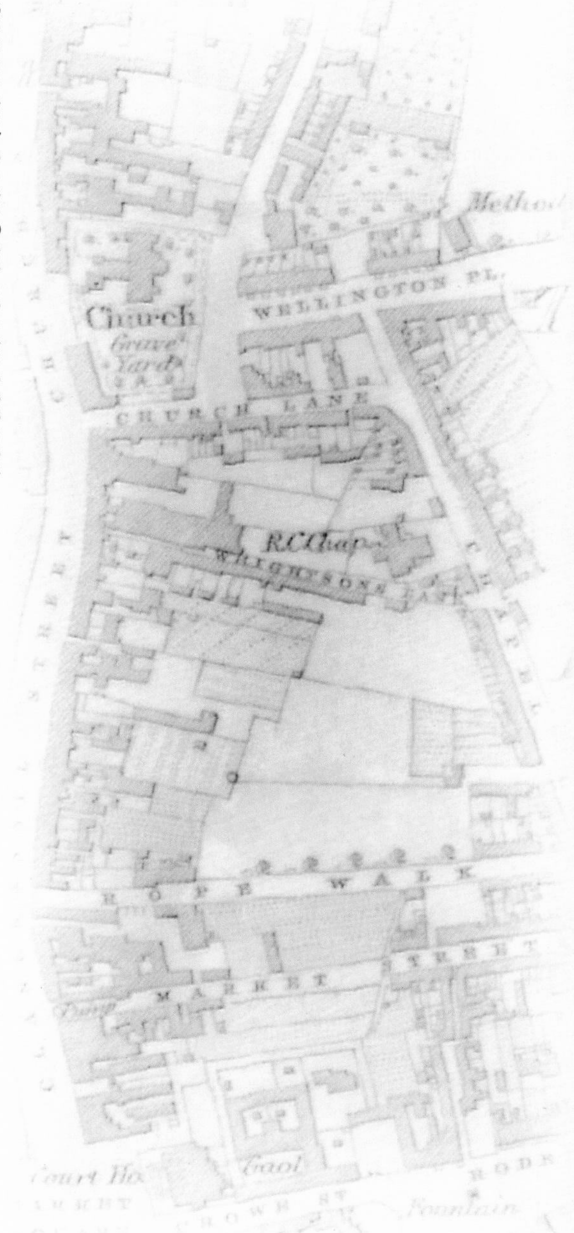

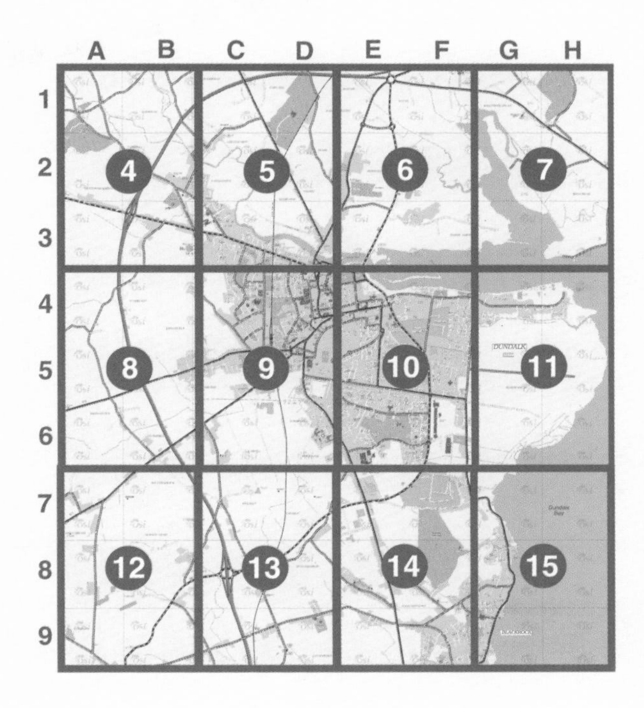

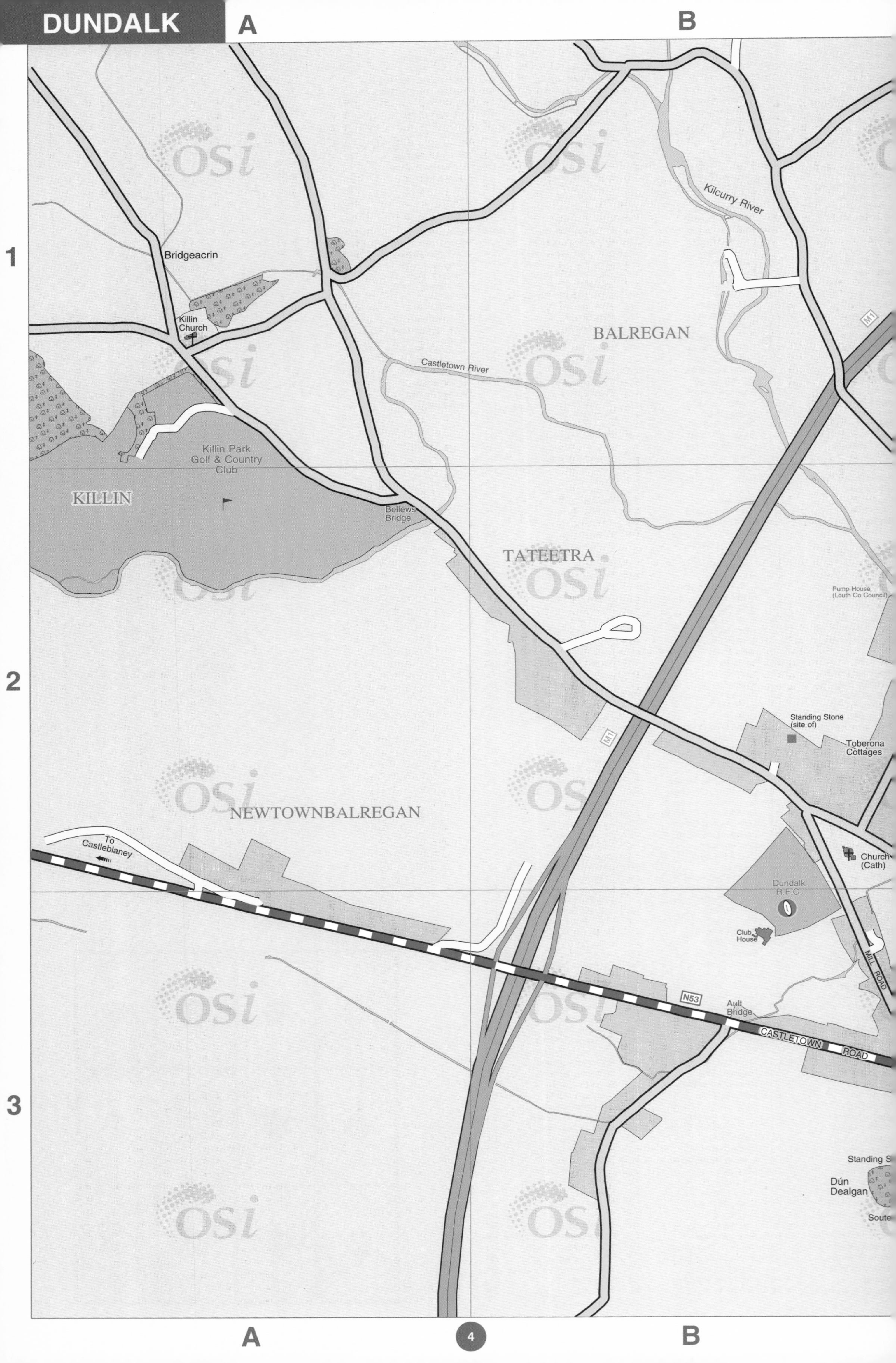
A
B
1
2
3
Bridgeacrin
Killin Church
Killin Park Golf & Country Club
KILLIN
Bellews Bridge
Castletown River
Kilcurry River
BALREGAN
TATEETRA
M1
Pump House (Louth Co Council)
Standing Stone (site of)
Toberona Cottages
NEWTOWNBALREGAN
To Castleblaney
Church (Cath)
Dundalk R.F.C.
Club House
MILL ROAD
N53
Ault Bridge
CASTLETOWN ROAD
Dún Dealgan
A
B

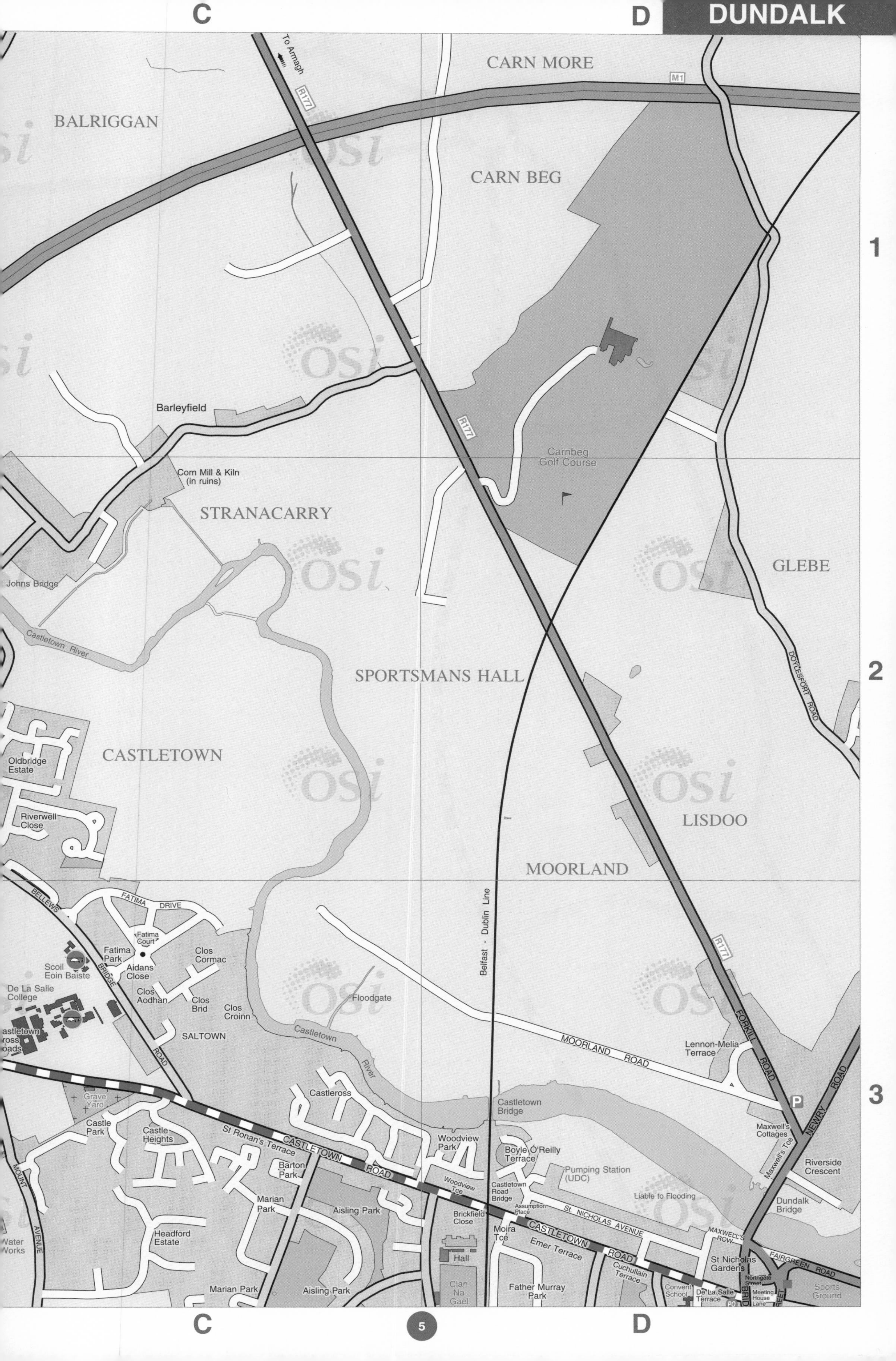
To Armagh
R177
CARN MORE
M1
BALRIGGAN
CARN BEG
1
Barleyfield
Carnbeg Golf Course
Corn Mill & Kiln (in ruins)
STRANACARRY
GLEBE
Johns Bridge
Castletown River
SPORTSMANS HALL
2
DOYLESFORT ROAD
CASTLETOWN
Oldbridge Estate
Riverwell Close
LISDOO
MOORLAND
BELLEWS BRIDGE ROAD
FATIMA DRIVE
Fatima Court
Fatima Park
Aidans Close
Clos Cormac
Clos Aodhan
Clos Brid
Clos Croinn
Scoil Eoin Baiste
De La Salle College
Castletown Cross Roads
SALTOWN
Belfast - Dublin Line
Floodgate
Castletown River
MOORLAND ROAD
FORKILL ROAD
Lennon-Melia Terrace
NEWRY ROAD
3
Grave Yard
Castle Park
Castle Heights
Castleross
Castletown Bridge
Maxwell's Cottages
Maxwell's Tce
St Ronan's Terrace
CASTLETOWN ROAD
Woodview Park
Boyle O'Reilly Terrace
Pumping Station (UDC)
Riverside Crescent
Barton Park
Woodview Tce
Castletown Road Bridge
Assumption Place
Liable to Flooding
Dundalk Bridge
MOUNT AVENUE
Marian Park
Aisling Park
Brickfield Close
ST. NICHOLAS AVENUE
MAXWELL'S ROW
Headford Estate
Moira Tce
Emer Terrace
Water Works
Hall
Cuchullain Terrace
St Nicholas Gardens
FAIRGREEN ROAD
Marian Park
Aisling Park
Clan Na Gael
Father Murray Park
Convent School
De La Salle Terrace
Northgate Street
Meeting House Lane
Sports Ground
BRIDGE STREET

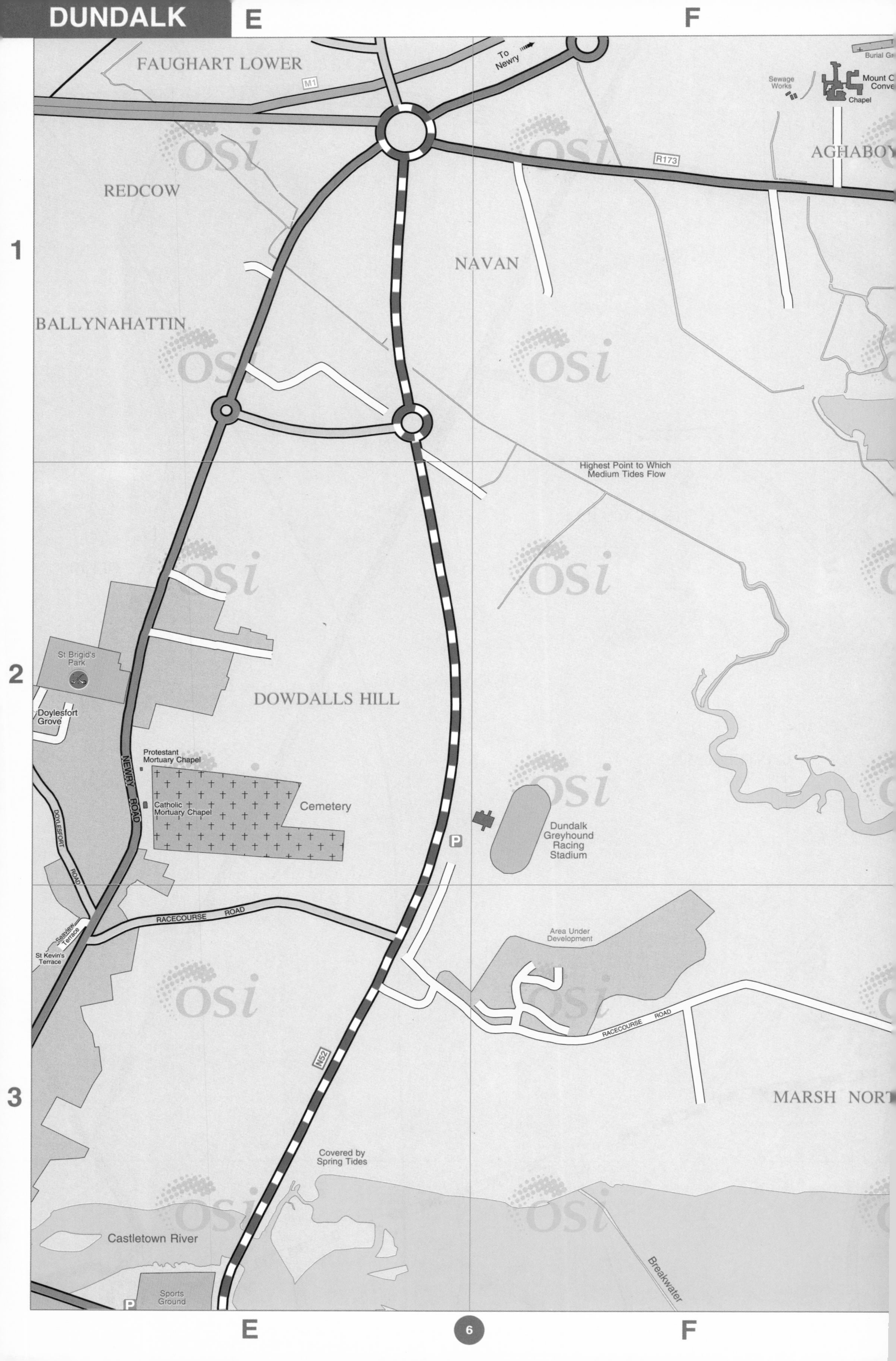
E
F
FAUGHART LOWER
M1
To Newry
Burial Gr
Sewage Works
Mount C
Conve
Chapel
REDCOW
R173
AGHABOY
NAVAN
BALLYNAHATTIN
Highest Point to Which Medium Tides Flow
St Brigid's Park
DOWDALLS HILL
Doylesfort Grove
Protestant Mortuary Chapel
NEWRY ROAD
DOYLESFORT ROAD
Catholic Mortuary Chapel
Cemetery
Dundalk Greyhound Racing Stadium
P
RACECOURSE ROAD
Seaview Terrace
St Kevin's Terrace
Area Under Development
RACECOURSE ROAD
N52
MARSH NORT
Covered by Spring Tides
Castletown River
Breakwater
Sports Ground
P
1
2
3

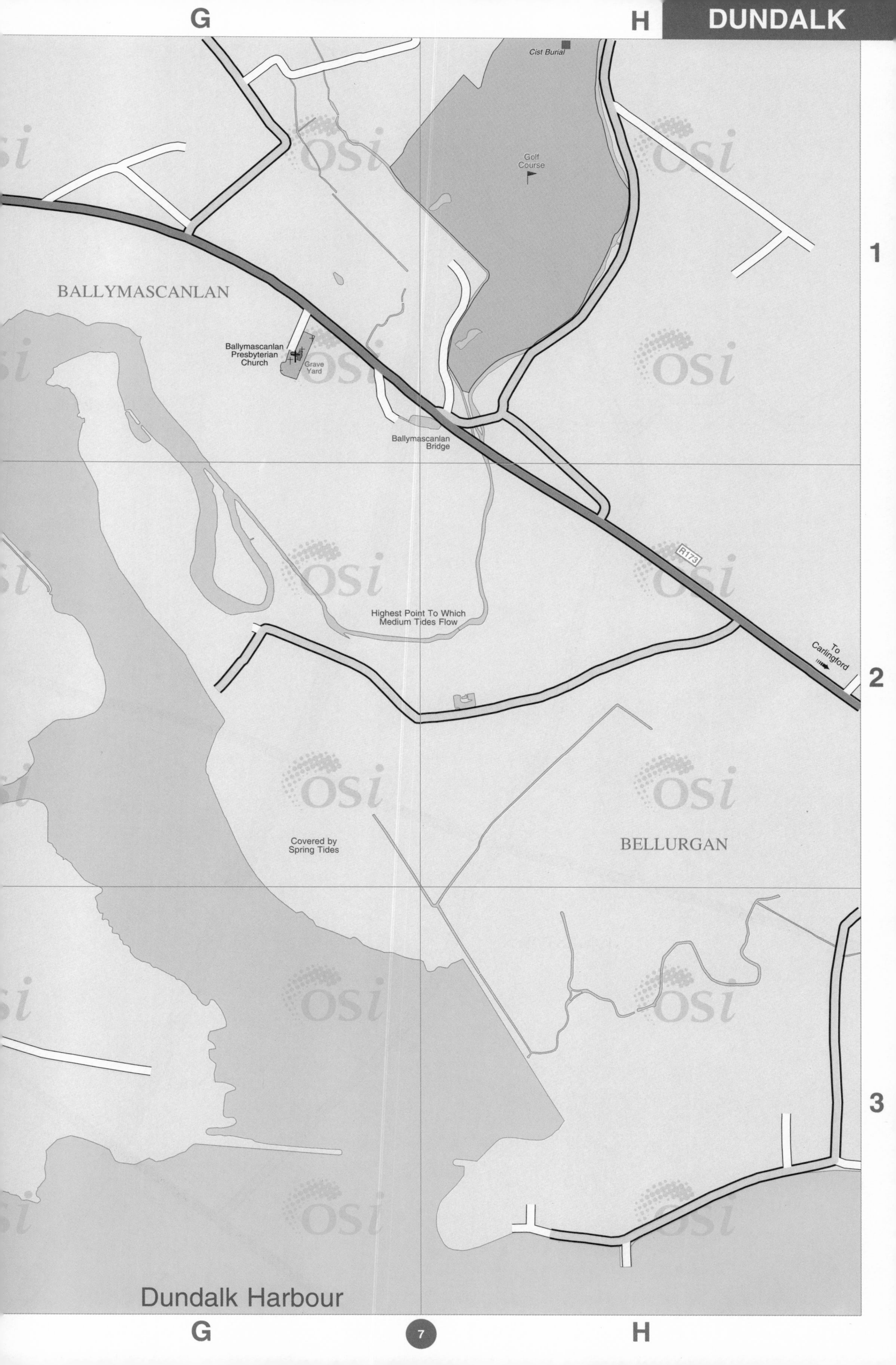
G
H
Cist Burial
Golf Course
1
BALLYMASCANLAN
Ballymascanlan Presbyterian Church
Grave Yard
Ballymascanlan Bridge
R173
Highest Point To Which Medium Tides Flow
To Carlingford
2
Covered by Spring Tides
BELLURGAN
3
Dundalk Harbour
G
H

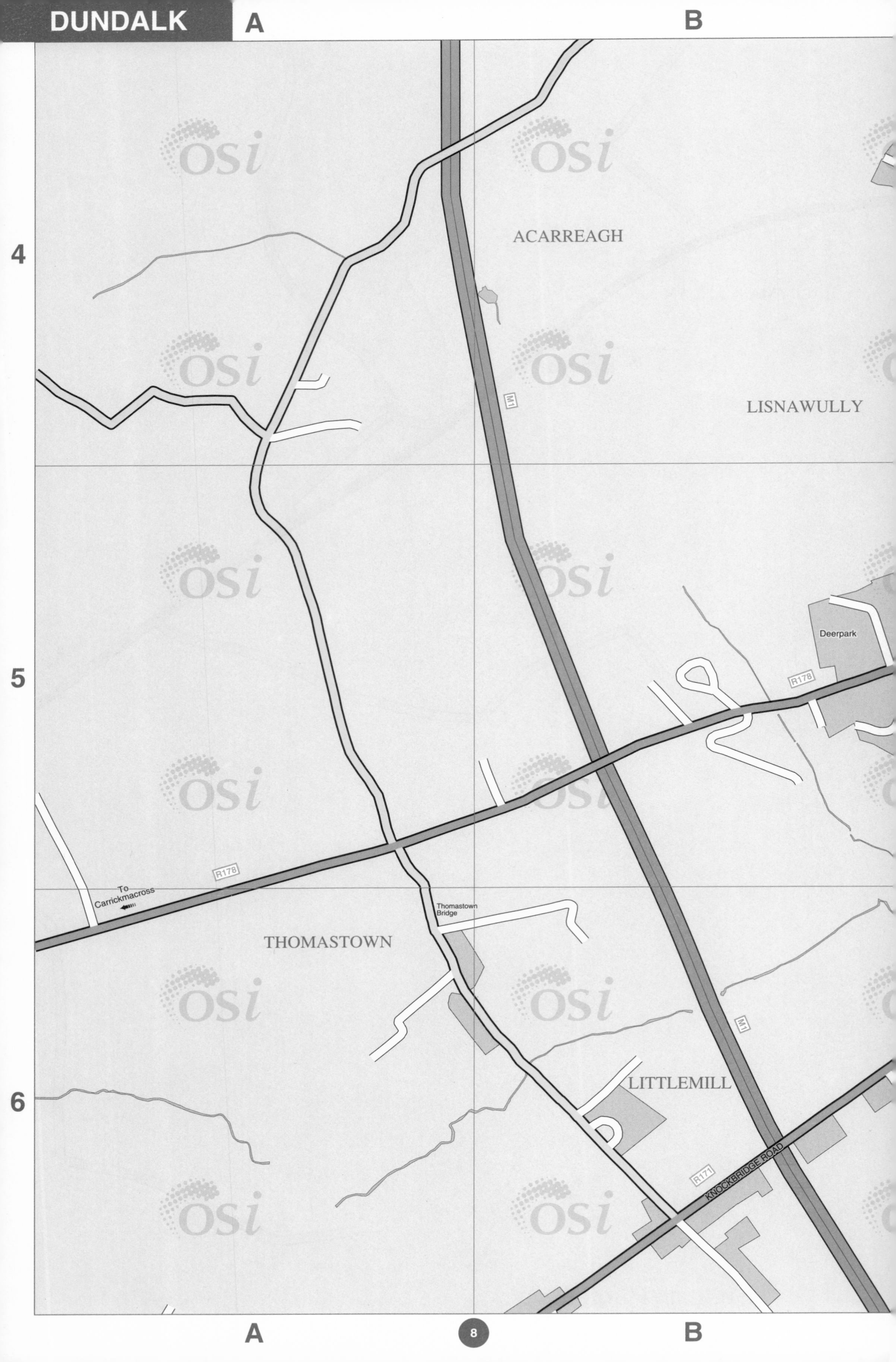
A
B
4
5
6
ACARREAGH
LISNAWULLY
M1
Deerpark
R178
To Carrickmacross
Thomastown Bridge
THOMASTOWN
LITTLEMILL
R171
KNOCKBRIDGE ROAD
A
B

C
D
4
5
6
Oakland Park
Farndreg Close
Farndreg Estate
Cedarwood Park
Beechmount Park
Clann Chullainn
Redeemer National School
Hall
St Brigid's School
Church Of The Holy Redeemer
BEECHMOUNT DRIVE
BÓTHAIR BLINNE
BÓTHAR BRÚ
CLONEEN DRIVE
DÚN MHIC CAINTE
RATH CONAILLE
ANNAVERNA DRIVE
Woodland Drive
MOUNT AVENUE
ARD EASMUIN ROAD
O'HANLON PARK WEST
CULHANE STREET
Hill View
O'HANLON STREET NORTH
O'HANLON PARK EAST
O'HANLON STREET SOUTH
LEGION AVENUE
MAC SWINEY STREET
LAURELS ROAD
Laurel Brook Gardens
Laurel Brook Close
Oliver Plunkett Park
DEMESNE ROAD
THE LONG WALK
Ice House Hill
Eircom Depot
Carroll Mead
PARK DRIVE
Park View
PARK AVENUE
Pearse Park
An Post Sorting Office
Hall
McENTEE AVENUE
Priory Villas
MULHOLLAND AVE
The Demesne
PARK VILLAS
Magnet Road
Brewery
Sports Field
Saint Malachy's National School
Saint Malachy's Church (Cath)
Hall
Clarke Station
Demesne Terrace
Carrickmacross Road Bridge
McDermott's Terrace
CARRICKMACROSS ROAD
ST DOMINICK'S PLACE
R178
Railway Terrace
Mounthamilton Close
Kincora Terrace
Dundalk Junction
St Malachy's Villas
The Crescent
ANNE STREET
St Anne's Court
MARY STREET
Wynne's Terrace
THOMAS STREET
VINCENT AVENUE
STAPLETON DRIVE
STAPLETON PLACE
DUBLIN STREET
HILL STREET
Parnell Park
Tennis Courts
Dundalk Grammar School
Sports Ground
ARDEE ROAD
Ardee Road Bridge
Sports Field
Oriel Park
Willow Grove
Rockmount Gardens
Hill Street Bridge
E.S.B. Depot
Sports Ground
Williamson's Place
PARK STREET
RIVER LANE
RAMPART LANE
RAMPART ROAD
FRANCIS STREET
EARL STREET
Market Square
Courthouse
Town Hall
CROWE STREET
Defenders Row
MARKET STREET
The Arches
BACHELORS WALK
Albert Place
UNION STREET
Christian Brothers Primary School
RUINN COLMCILLE
Coláiste Rís
YORKE STREET
CHAPEL
Wellington Place
St Mary's Church
NICHOLAS STREET
St Nicholas Church (C of I)
St Mary's College (Sec)
College Court
WOLFE TONE TERRACE
Bridge Water Mews
St Nicholas N.S.
FAIRGREEN ROW
LINENHALL STREET
CHURCH STREET
CLANBRASSIL STREET
Church of St Nicholas (Cath)
De La Salle S.C.
JOHN STREET
St Phillip's N.S.
PATRICK STREET
PHILIP STREET
St John's Court
Griffith Court
Bus Depot
THE LONG WALK
MOUNTHAMILTON
Mounthamilton
Engineering Works
Ardee Terrace
ARDEE LANE
BROOK STREET
Bus Depot
R171
Hill's Lane
THE LONG AVENUE
Regan's Terrace
Gosling's Terrace
Dunmore
Line Terrace
Hughes Park
Mourne View
Lady's Well
Lady Well Terrace
DUBLIN ROAD
R132
Balmer's Bog
PRIORLAND GARDENS
PRIORLAND ROAD
TOWNPARKS
Priorland Grove
Mortuary
Chapel
St Oliver Plunkett Hospital
Louth County Hospital
Rath Park
Church (Disused)
FAIRHILL
PRIORLAND
Langfield

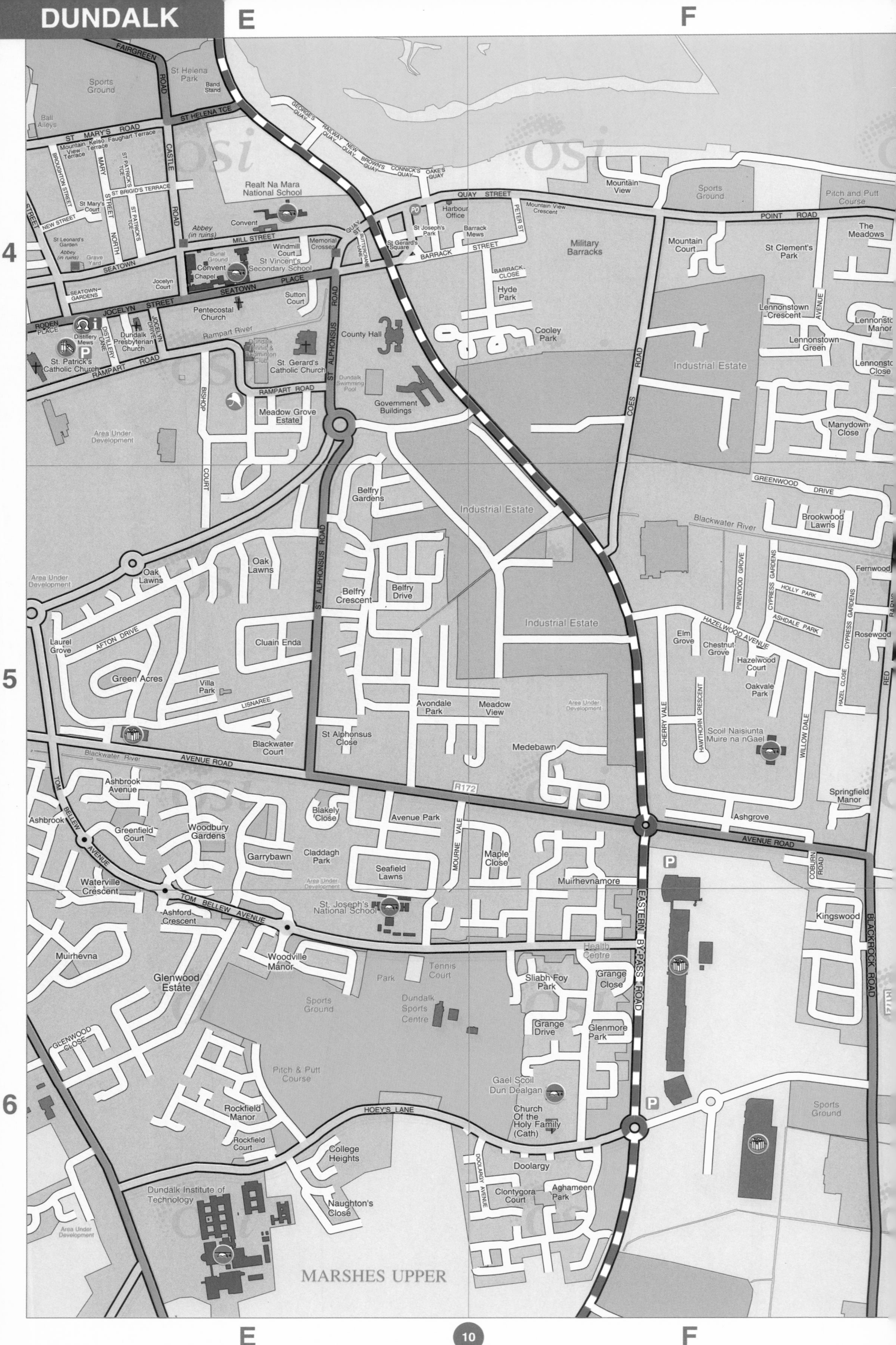
E
F
4
5
6
Sports Ground
St Helena Park
Band Stand
Ball Alleys
FAIRGREEN ROAD
ST HELENA TCE
ST MARY'S ROAD
CASTLE ROAD
Realt Na Mara National School
Convent
Abbey (in ruins)
MILL STREET
Windmill Court
Memorial Crosses
Convent Chapel
St Vincent's Secondary School
SEATOWN PLACE
Sutton Court
Pentecostal Church
JOCELYN STREET
Rampart River
St. Gerard's Catholic Church
Dundalk Presbyterian Church
Distillery Mews
St. Patrick's Catholic Church
RAMPART ROAD
County Hall
Government Buildings
Dundalk Swimming Pool
Meadow Grove Estate
BISHOP COURT
ST ALPHONSUS ROAD
GEORGE'S QUAY
RAILWAY QUAY
NEW QUAY
BROWN'S QUAY
CONNICK'S QUAY
OAKE'S QUAY
QUAY STREET
Harbour Office
St Joseph's Park
Barrack Mews
St Gerard's Square
BARRACK STREET
PETER ST
Mountain View Crescent
Mountain View
Military Barracks
BARRACK CLOSE
Hyde Park
Cooley Park
Sports Ground
Pitch and Putt Course
POINT ROAD
Mountain Court
St Clement's Park
The Meadows
Lennonstown Crescent
Lennonstown Green
Industrial Estate
COES ROAD
Manydown Close
GREENWOOD DRIVE
Brookwood Lawns
Blackwater River
Fernwood
HOLLY PARK
ASHDALE PARK
HAZELWOOD AVENUE
Elm Grove
Chestnut Grove
Hazelwood Court
Oakvale Park
Rosewood
Scoil Naisiunta Muire na nGael
CHERRY VALE
HAWTHORN CRESCENT
WILLOW DALE
Springfield Manor
Ashgrove
AVENUE ROAD
Belfry Gardens
Belfry Crescent
Belfry Drive
Industrial Estate
Oak Lawns
Area Under Development
Laurel Grove
AFTON DRIVE
Cluain Enda
Green Acres
Villa Park
LISNAREE
Blackwater Court
St Alphonsus Close
Avondale Park
Meadow View
Medebawn
R172
Ashbrook Avenue
Ashbrook
Woodbury Gardens
Greenfield Court
TOM BELLEW AVENUE
Garrybawn
Blakely Close
Avenue Park
Claddagh Park
Seafield Lawns
MOURNE VALE
Maple Close
Muirhevnamore
Waterville Crescent
Ashford Crescent
St. Joseph's National School
EASTERN BY-PASS ROAD
COBURN ROAD
Kingswood
BLACKROCK ROAD
Muirhevna
Glenwood Estate
Woodville Manor
Tennis Court
Park
Health Centre
Sliabh Foy Park
Grange Close
Sports Ground
Dundalk Sports Centre
Grange Drive
Glenmore Park
GLENWOOD CLOSE
Pitch & Putt Course
Gael Scoil Dun Dealgan
Church Of the Holy Family (Cath)
Rockfield Manor
Rockfield Court
HOEY'S LANE
College Heights
Doolargy
DOOLARGY AVENUE
Clontygora Court
Aghameen Park
Dundalk Institute of Technology
Naughton's Close
MARSHES UPPER
Sports Ground

G
H
4
5
6
Soldier's Point
Sports Ground
Suil Na Mara
LOWER POINT ROAD
Seacrest Manor
Area Under Development
Water View
Area Under Development
Area Under Development
Riverside Drive
Blackwater River
Covered By Spring Tides
SHORE ROAD
MARSH SOUTH
Covered By Spring Tides
Covered By Spring Tides
G
H

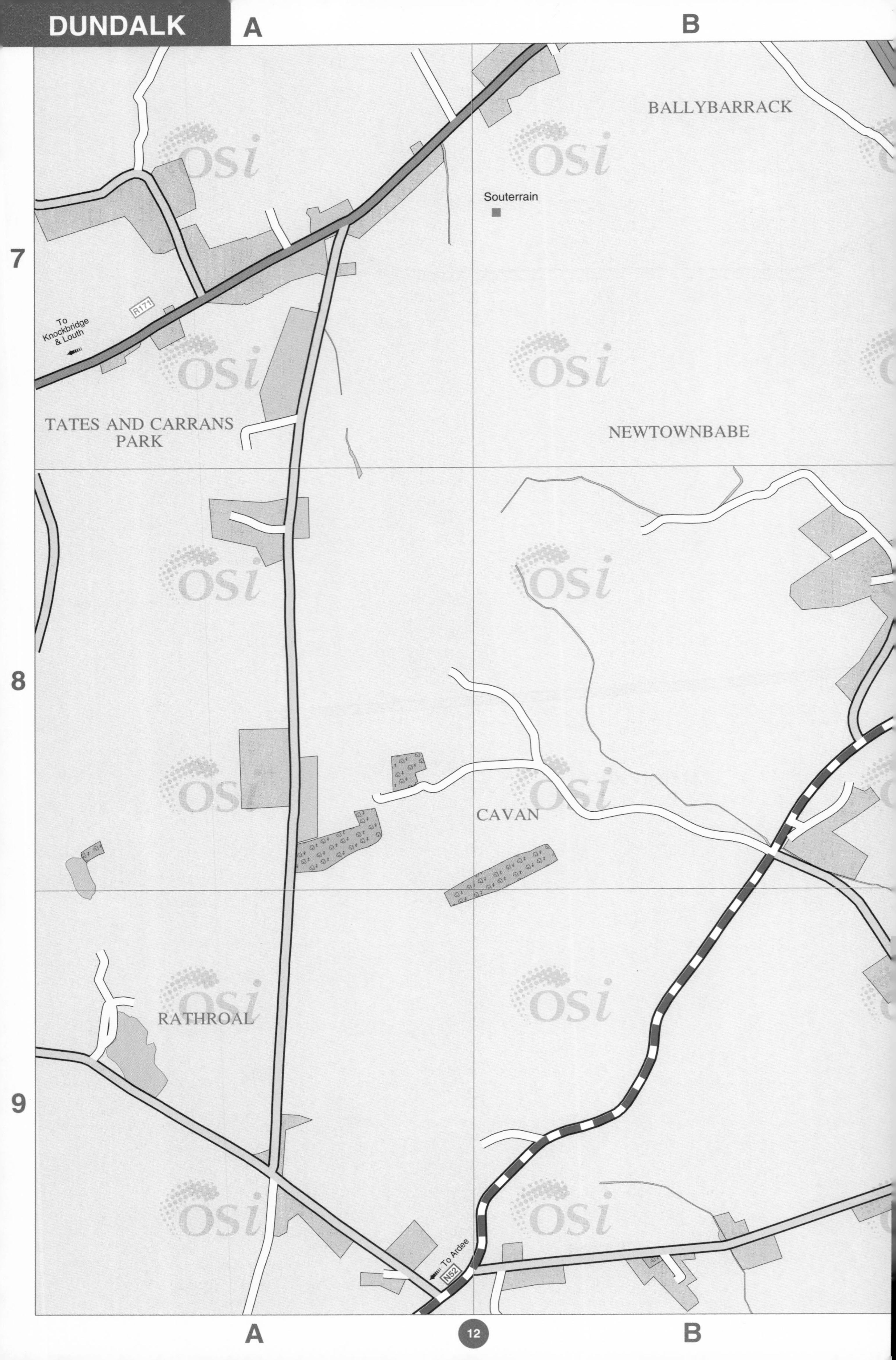
A
B
7
8
9
BALLYBARRACK
Souterrain
R171
To
Knockbridge
& Louth
TATES AND CARRANS
PARK
NEWTOWNBABE
CAVAN
RATHROAL
To Ardee
N52
A
B

C
D
7
8
9
Grave Yard (Disused)
Souterrain
Souterrain
KILLALLY
CRUMLIN
M1
Crumlin Bridge
N52
MULLAGHARLIN
BSTOWN
Haynestown Bridge
MULLAGHARLIN ROAD
Brookfield
St. Fursey's National School
Geraldine's GAA Club
MARLBOG ROAD
Clermont Bridge
St. Paul's Church (C of I)
Castle (In Ruins)
HAYNESTOWN
Dublin - Belfast Line
To Drogheda & Dublin
Paddock Wood
UNMAHON
C
D

E
F
7
8
9
Finnabair Industrial Estate
Halting Site
Souterrain
EASTERN BY-PASS ROAD
N52
DUBLIN ROAD
MULLAHARLIN ROAD
The Loakers
BOTHAR MAOL
R132
Dundalk Golf Club
Club House
Haggardstown Church (Cath)
Windmill Stump
CHAPEL ROAD
The Links
Castle (Site of)
OLD GOLF LINKS ROAD
TUITE'S LANE
HAMILTON DRIVE
Church (In Ruins)
Grave Yard
ROCK VILLE
THE ROCK
Sandy Grove Close
Gort Na Glaise
HAGGARDSTOWN
Mayfield Drive
SEAFIELD ROAD
Rathmount Estate
Ard Na Mara
Springfield
Nursing Home
Ard Shee
Wallace Cove
CARRAIG ARD
ST. FURSEY'S TERRACE
DUBLIN ROAD
Bellfield View
Clermont Estate
Clermont Park
R172
COCKLE HILL
E
F

G
H
7
8
9
Dundalk Bay
Highest Point To Which Medium Tides Flow
R172
BLACKROCK ROAD
Village Green
NEW GOLF LINKS LANE
BIRCHES LANE
Blackrock Cove
Marine Drive
Marine View
The Square
Rockmount
Tennis Court
Marine Court
Marine Avenue
Marine Crescent
SANDYMOUNT
Sandymount
Sandymount Drive
Water Works
The Orchard
ROCK ROAD
The Meadows
THE ROCK ROAD
FAIRVIEW
ELM PARK
CHAPEL PASS
Church of St.Oliver Plunkett (Cath)
Sandfield Gardens
Church Park
MAIN STREET
Oliver Plunkett National School
SANDY LANE
P
BEECH PARK
PO
Blackrock
Ascal Emer
Ferns Cove
THE FERNS
South End
Wavecrest Drive
Seafield Gardens
Slip

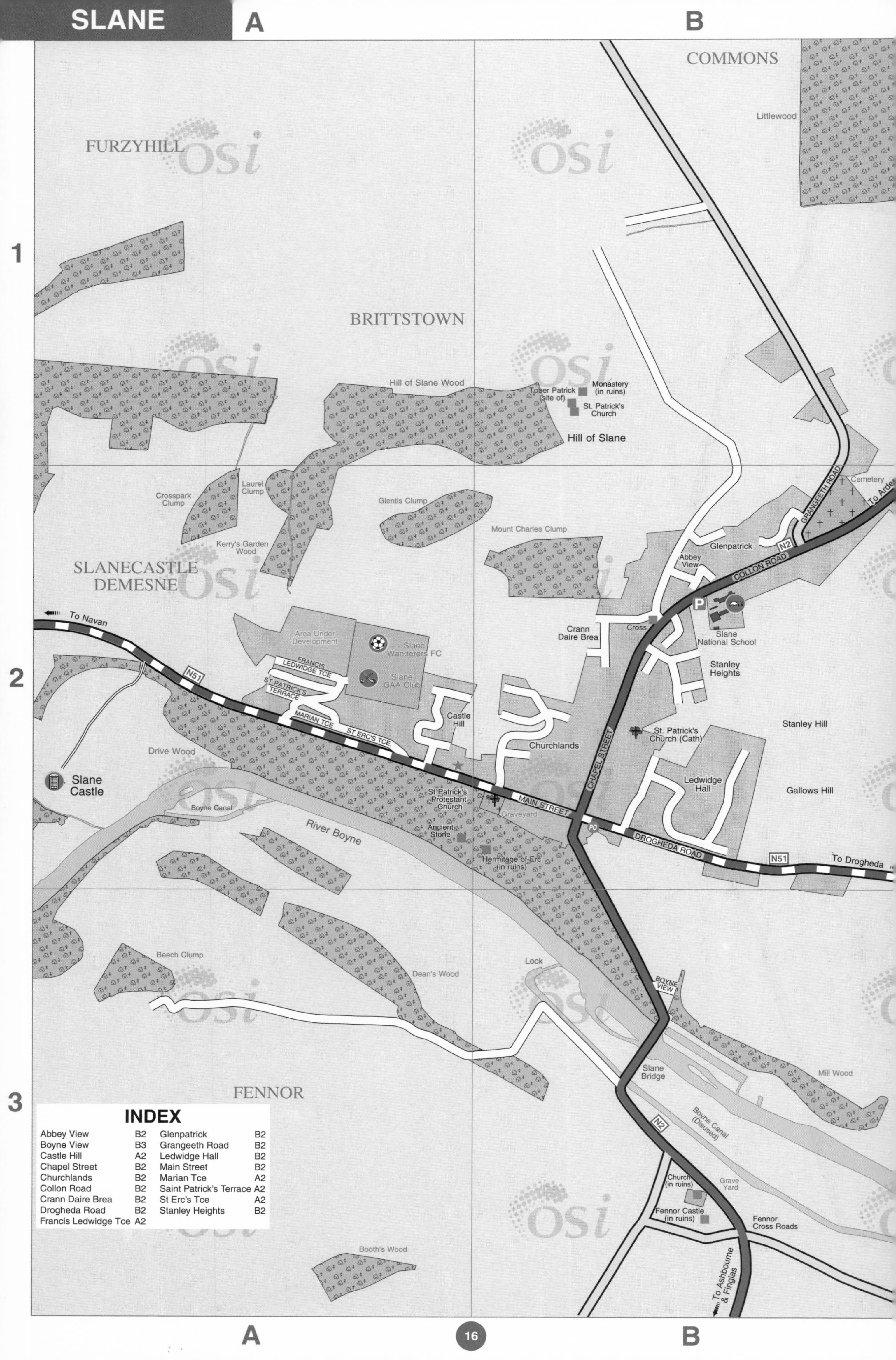

INDEX

Abbey View	B2	Glenpatrick	B2
Boyne View	B3	Grangeeth Road	B2
Castle Hill	A2	Ledwidge Hall	B2
Chapel Street	B2	Main Street	B2
Churchlands	B2	Marian Tce	A2
Collon Road	B2	Saint Patrick's Terrace	A2
Crann Daire Brea	B2	St Erc's Tce	A2
Drogheda Road	B2	Stanley Heights	B2
Francis Ledwidge Tce	A2		

INDEX

Acorn Way F4
An Craobhin Terrace D3
Anneville Crescent D3
Ard Rí E5
Ardan an Bothar Ghlais E2
Ascal A Dó E2
Ascal A hAon E2
Ascal A Trí E2
Ascal Brugha D3
Ashdale F4
Ashfield Close D3
Ashfield Crescent D3
Ashfield Green D3
Ashfield Heights D3
Ashfield View D3
Ashling Green D3
Ashling Grove C3
Aston Village F2
Autumn Way F4
Avondale F4
Ballast Quay E3
Ballsgrove Estate D4
Bally Park E2
Ballymakenny Road E1
Barley Cove F4
Barrack Street E4
Beaubec F4
Beaulieu Estate F2
Beaulieu Mews F3
Beech Grove Terrace D2
Beechgrove Crescent E2
Beechmount Avenue F4
Beechwood Close F2
Beechwood Drive F2
Beechwood Drive C4
Belvedere C3
Bessexwell Lane E3
Blackbush Avenue E4
Blackbush Lane E4
Bolton Street D3
Bothar Brugha D3
Bottle Lane D4
Boyle O'Reilly Terrace D2
Boyne Business Park F2
Boyne Court E3
Boyne Hall B3
Boyne Lodge C3
Boyne Meadow B3
Boyne Terrace E3
Boyne Valley Cottages C3
Boyne View D3
Bredin Court E3
Bredin Street E3
Brickfields D3
Bridge View E2
Broadmeadows E2
Brookside Lodge E2
Brookville E2
Bryanstown Close E4
Bryanstown Court E4
Bryanstown Manor E4
Bryanstown Village F4
Buck House Lane E2
Cairnes Court G4
Carmelite Cottages E3
Castle Manor E2
Castlewood G4
Cearnog Brugha D3
Cedarfield Close C4
Cedarfield Close C4
Cedarwood C4
Cement Road C3
Cherrybrook Drive D4
Cherrymount D4
Cherrywood Close F2
Cherrywood Drive F2
Chesnut Grove F2
Church Lane E3
Clinton's Lane E4
College Rise E2
Congress Avenue D4
Constitution Hill E3
Coolagh Lodge E4
Coolagh Well E4
Copper Close F4
Cord Terrace E3
Cormorant Street F2
Corporation Cottages D4
Corry's Hill E4
Cromwell's Lane E4
Cromwell's Mount E4
Cross Lane D2
Crushrod Lane E3
Custom House Quay E3
Dale Walk E4
De Lacy Bridge E3
Dominick Street D3
Donore Avenue D4
Donore Ind. Estate C5
Donore Road C4
Downey's Cottages D3
Dublin Road E4
Duke Street D3
Duleek Gate D4
Duleek Street E4
Dyer Street D3
Earlwood E3
Elmwood D4
Elmwood Close F2
Fair Green D3
Fair Street D3
Five Oaks F4
Five Oaks Village F5
Flaxmill Lane E2
Forest Edge F4
Forest Grange E2
Forest Hill E2
Forest Park E2
Forest View G4
Fountain Cottages C3
Fountain Hill C3
Fox Hill F4
Francis Street E3
George's Street D3
Georgian Close D3
Glenmore Drive E3
Glenview E3
Grange Rath G5
Grange Rise E2
Gravel Walk D3
Green Lane D3
Green View Cottages E4
Greenhills Road E3
Halpin's Terrace D4
Hand Street E3
Hardman's Gardens D3
Harmony Heights F2
Harvest Way F4
Haymarket D4
Hazel lane E4
Heron Street F1
Highfield D4
Hillbrook Drive D4
Hillview C3
Horse Lane D3
James Street E4
John Paul Court D3
King Street E3
Knockbrack Downs C5
Laburnum Drive F2
Laburnam Square D3
Laburnum Turret D3
Lagavoreen Manor D5
Laurel Court D4
Laurel Mews E3
Leafy Haven F4
Legavoureen Park E4
Leyland Place D3
Limetree Avenue E2
Longwood F4
Lourdes Square D3
Magdalene Street D3
Maple Drive E3
Marian Close E3
Marian Court D4
Marian Park D4
Marley Court C4
Marley's Lane C4
Marsh Road E3
Martello Village E4
Mary Street E4
Matson Lodge E2
Matthew's Lane C4
Mayfield D2
Mayoralty Street E3
McEvoy's Lane D4
McGrath's Lane F4
Meadow View E4
Meat Market D3
Mell Lane C3
Mellifont Park C2
Melrose Avenue G4
Merchant's Quay E3
Mill Lane D3
Mill Row D3
Millhaven E2
Millmount Abbey E5
Millmount Square E4
Moneymore Estate D2
Moneymore Lane D2
Moores Lane D3
Moran's Terrace D4
Mount Auburn E4
Mount Sandford E2
Mount St. Oliver D4
Newfield Estate E2
Newfoundwell Road E2
Newtown Road F2
North Quay E3
North Road D2
North Strand E3
Nun's Walk E3
Oak Drive D4
Oak Drive D4
Oaklawns D3
Oakwood Park F2
Oaten Vale F4
Old Abbey Lane D3
Old Corn Market Hill E4
Oldbridge Estate B3
Oulster's Lane E3
Palace Row E3
Paradise Place E3
Park Avenue G5
Park Close G4
Park Court H4
Park Crescent G5
Park Drive G5
Park Green H4
Park Hill H4
Park Lane G4
Park Lawn G5
Park Row G4
Park Square G4
Park View G4
Park Way H4
Park Wood G4
Patrick Street D3
Patrickswell Lane D3
Pearse Park E3
Peter Street D3
Pine Hamlet E4
Pinewood F3
Platin Road D4
Poorhouse Lane E4
Priest's Lane D4
Radharc Na Pairce D3
Railway Terrace F4
Rathmullan Park C4
Rathmullan Road C3
Redshank Court F1
Regent Place E3
Ricardo Terrace E3
River Court C3
River View C3
Riverbank Estate B3
Rockville E4
Rope Walk D3
Rose Hill Cottages E3
Rosevale E4
Rowan Heights C4
Sampson's Lane E4
Sandyford Terrace E3
Scarlet Crescent E3
Scholes Lane D3
Shady Grove F4
Shamrock Villas E2
Shelduck Street F1
Ship Street E3
Shop Street E3
Shrewsbury Manor F3
Silk Park D4
Silverstream Avenue G4
Simcocks Lane D3
Singleton Cottages C3
South Quay E3
St Joseph's Terrace C3
St Lawrence's Terrace E3
St. Bridget's Terrace E3
St. Catherine's Terrace E3
St. Finian's Park C4
St. Laurence's Drive D2
St. Laurence's Park D2
St. Lawrence Street E3
St. Magdalene Terrace E3
St. Mary's Cottages E4
St. Mary's Villas E4
St. Patrick's Cottages E4
St. Peter's Terrace D3
St. Theresa's Terrace E3
Stameen G4
Stameen Lawns G4
Steam Packet Quay E3
Stockwell Lane D3
Strand Cottages E3
Strand Road F3
Sunday's Gate D3
Sunhill F4
Sunnyside Cottages E4
Sycamore Close F2
Teal Street F1
Termon Abbey F2
The Avenue B4
The Avenue (Millmount Abbey) E5
The Boulevard G4
The Cairns F4
The Close B4
The Close (Millmount Abbey) E5
The Court B4
The Crescent B4
The Crescent (Millmount Abbey) E5
The Dale (Riverbank) B3
The Dale E4
The Downs B4
The Drive (Riverbank) B3
The Drive B4
The Drive (Millmount Abbey) E5
The Green (Riverbank) B3
The Green (Millmount Abbey) E4
The Green B4
The Lawn B4
The Mall E3
The Moorings E3
The Oaks E5
The Park (Riverbank) B3
The Park E4
The Park (Millmount Abbey) E4
The Priory F2
The Square (Riverbank) B3
The Sycamores F3
The View (Riverbank) B3
The View (Millmount Abbey) E5
The Way B3
Toberboice Lane C3
Tredagh Close C4
Tredagh View C4
Trinity Gardens D3
Trinity Street D3
Twenties Lane D2
Watery Hill D4
Weaver's Way F4
Weirhope F3
Wellington Quay D3
West Street D3
Westcourt F3
Westwood F4
Wheaton Hall F4
Whitethorn D2
William Street E3
Willow Grove C3
Windmill Court D2
Windmill Road D2
Woodford F4
Woodgrange G5
Woodgrove F4
Woodlane F4
Woodview F4
Yellowbatter E2

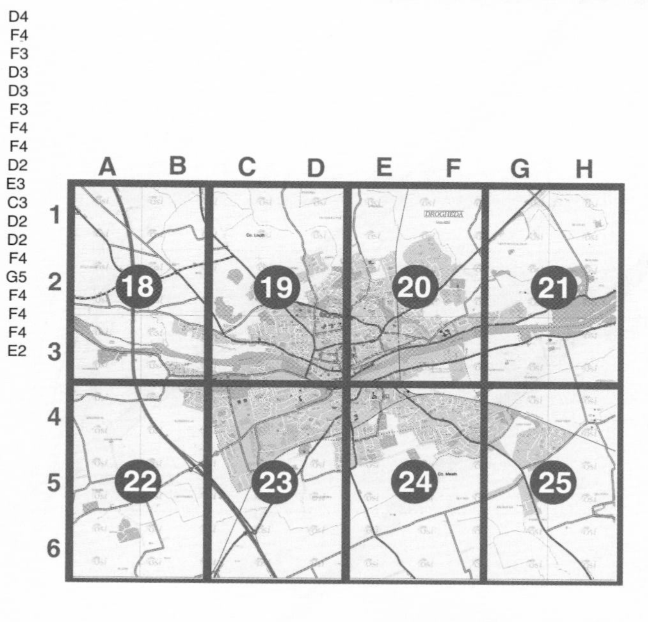

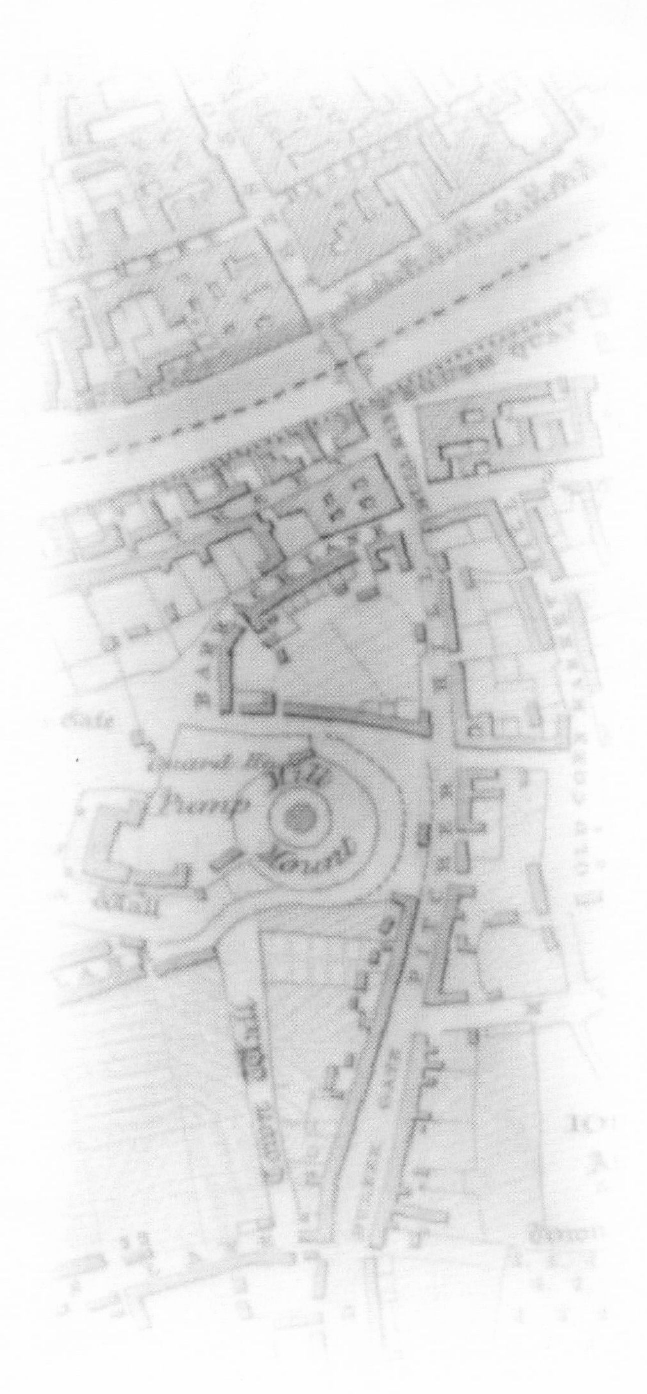

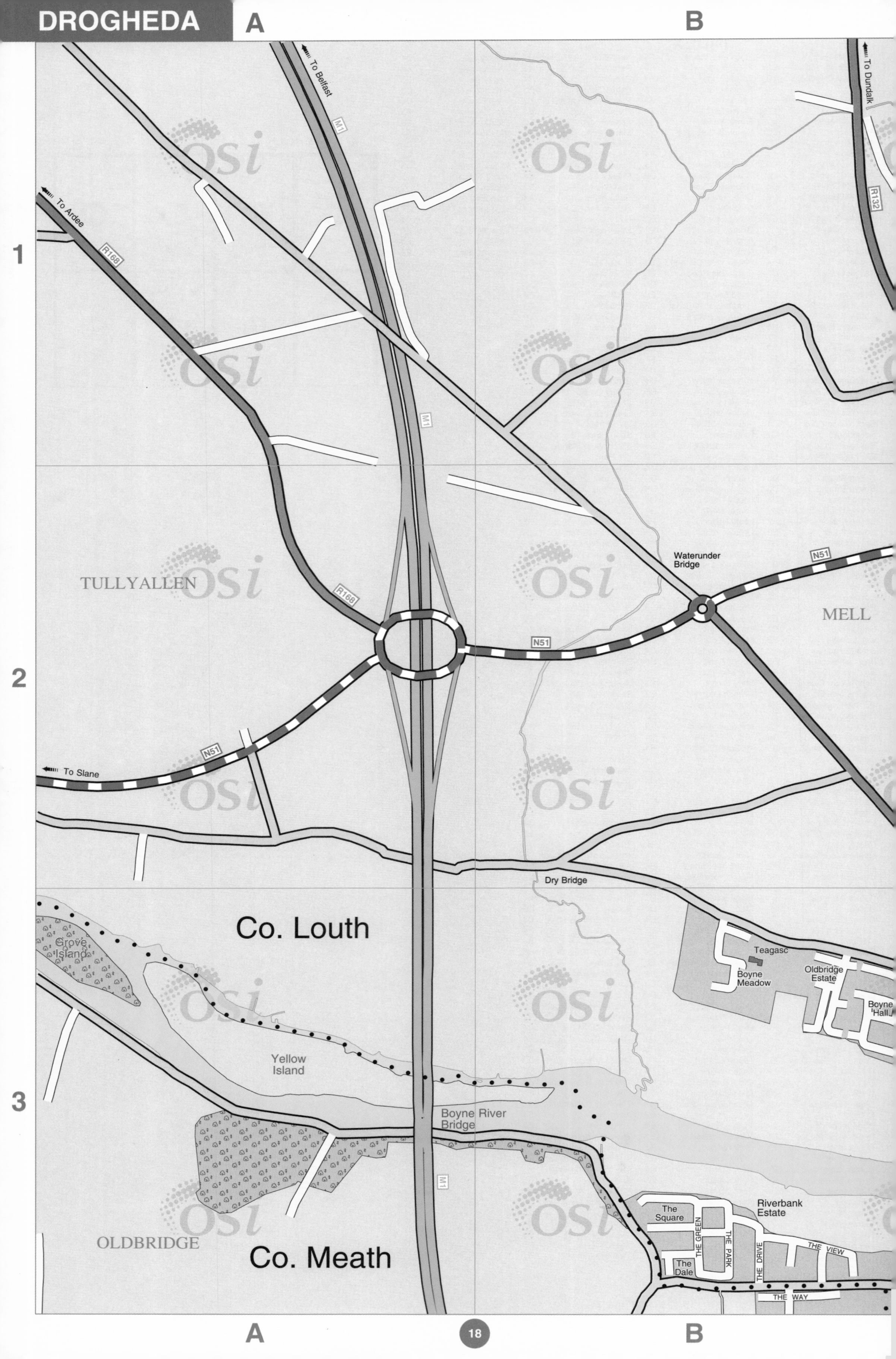
A
B
1
2
3
To Belfast
M1
To Dundalk
R132
To Ardee
R168
TULLYALLEN
R168
Waterunder Bridge
N51
MELL
N51
N51
To Slane
Dry Bridge
Co. Louth
Grove Island
Teagasc
Boyne Meadow
Oldbridge Estate
Boyne Hall
Yellow Island
Boyne River Bridge
M1
Riverbank Estate
The Square
THE GREEN
THE PARK
THE DRIVE
THE VIEW
The Dale
THE WAY
OLDBRIDGE
Co. Meath
A
B

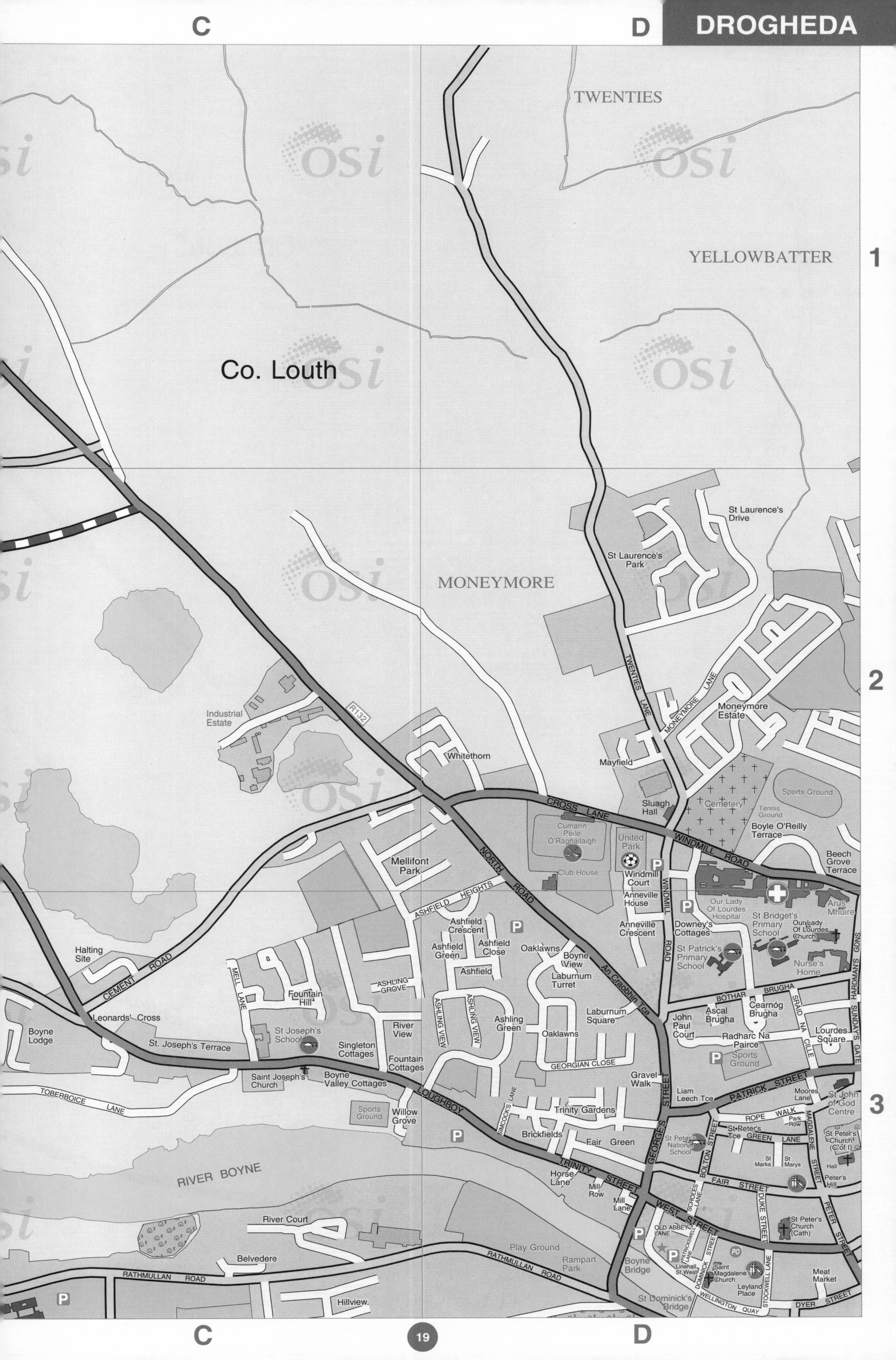
C
D
TWENTIES
YELLOWBATTER
1
Co. Louth
St Laurence's Drive
St Laurence's Park
MONEYMORE
2
TWENTIES LANE
MONEYMORE LANE
Moneymore Estate
Industrial Estate
R132
Whitethorn
Mayfield
Sports Ground
Cemetery
Sluagh Hall
Tennis Ground
CROSS LANE
Cumann Peile O'Raghallaigh
United Park
Boyle O'Reilly Terrace
WINDMILL ROAD
Beech Grove Terrace
Mellifont Park
NORTH ROAD
Club House
Windmill Court
Anneville House
Our Lady Of Lourdes Hospital
St Bridget's Primary School
Ard Mhuire
ASHFIELD HEIGHTS
Ashfield Crescent
Anneville Crescent
Downey's Cottages
Our Lady Of Lourdes Church
Ashfield Green
Ashfield Close
Oaklawns
Boyne View
St Patrick's Primary School
Nurse's Home
HARDMAN'S GDNS
Halting Site
CEMENT ROAD
MELL LANE
Ashfield
Laburnum Turret
ASHLING GROVE
WINDMILL ROAD
Fountain Hill
ASHLING VIEW
ASHLING VIEW
An Creaobhin Tce
BOTHAR BRUGHA
Ashling Green
Laburnum Square
Ascal Brugha
Cearnóg Brugha
SRAID NA CILLE
SUNDAY'S GATE
Leonards' Cross
John Paul Court
Lourdes Square
Boyne Lodge
St Joseph's School
River View
Oaklawns
Radharc Na Pairce
St. Joseph's Terrace
Singleton Cottages
Fountain Cottages
GEORGIAN CLOSE
Sports Ground
Gravel Walk
Saint Joseph's Church
Boyne Valley Cottages
Liam Leech Tce
PATRICK STREET
Moores Lane
St John of God Centre
3
TOBERBOICE LANE
LOUGHBOY
SIMCOCK'S LANE
Trinity Gardens
ROPE WALK
Park Row
Sports Ground
Willow Grove
GEORGE'S STREET
St Peters National School
St Peter's Tce
GREEN LANE
MAGDALENE STREET
St Peter's Church (C of I)
Brickfields
Fair Green
BOLTON STREET
St Marks
St Marys
Hall
RIVER BOYNE
TRINITY STREET
Horse Lane
Mill Row
FAIR STREET
Peter's Hill
Mill Lane
SCHOLES LANE
DUKE STREET
WEST STREET
River Court
OLD ABBEY LANE
PATRICKSWELL LANE
St Peter's Church (Cath)
PETER STREET
Play Ground
PO
Belvedere
Rampart Park
STOCKWELL LANE
RATHMULLAN ROAD
RATHMULLAN ROAD
Boyne Bridge
Linenhall St West
DOMINICK STREET
Saint Magdalene's Church
Leyland Place
Meat Market
Hillview
St Dominick's Bridge
WELLINGTON QUAY
DYER STREET
C
D

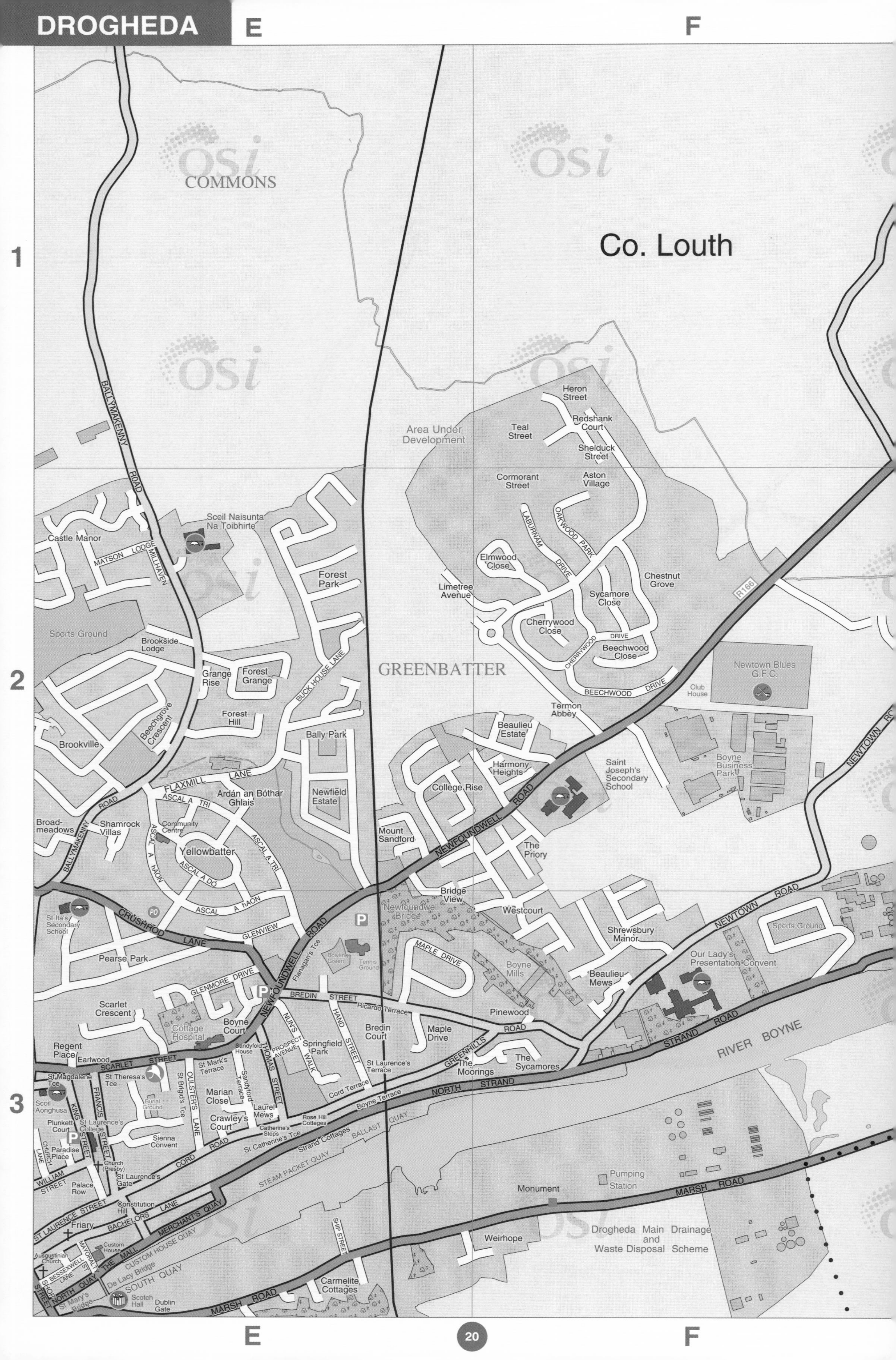
Co. Louth
COMMONS
GREENBATTER
Area Under Development
Heron Street
Redshank Court
Teal Street
Shelduck Street
Cormorant Street
Aston Village
Laburnam Drive
Oakwood Park
Elmwood Close
Chestnut Grove
Limetree Avenue
Sycamore Close
Cherrywood Close
Cherrywood Drive
Beechwood Close
Beechwood Drive
Newtown Blues G.F.C.
Club House
R166
Termon Abbey
Beaulieu Estate
Harmony Heights
College Rise
Saint Joseph's Secondary School
Boyne Business Park
Newtown Road
Mount Sandford
Newfoundwell Road
The Priory
Bridge View
Newfoundwell Bridge
Westcourt
Shrewsbury Manor
Sports Ground
Our Lady's Presentation Convent
Maple Drive
Boyne Mills
Beaulieu Mews
Pinewood
Strand Road
River Boyne
Scoil Naisunta Na Toibhirte
Castle Manor
Matson Lodge
Millhaven
Forest Park
Ballymakenny Road
Sports Ground
Brookside Lodge
Grange Rise
Forest Grange
Buck House Lane
Beechgrove Crescent
Forest Hill
Bally Park
Brookville
Flaxmill Lane
Ardán an Bóthar Ghlais
Newfield Estate
Broad-meadows
Shamrock Villas
Community Centre
Ascal a Tri
Ascal a hAon
Yellowbatter
Ascal a Do
St Ita's Secondary School
Crushrod Lane
Glenview
Flanagan's Tce
Bowling Green
Tennis Ground
Pearse Park
Glenmore Drive
Bredin Street
Ricardo Terrace
Scarlet Crescent
Cottage Hospital
Boyne Court
Nuns Walk
Prospect Avenue
Springfield Park
Hand Street
Bredin Court
Maple Drive
Greenhills Road
The Moorings
The Sycamores
Regent Place
Earlwood
Scarlet Street
St Magdalene Tce
St Theresa's Tce
Sandyfold House
St Mark's Terrace
St Brigid's Tce
Oulsters Lane
Sandyford Terrace
Thomas Street
St Laurence's Terrace
Cord Terrace
Boyne Terrace
North Strand
Scoil Aonghusa
King Street
Francis Street
Burial Ground
Marian Close
Laurel Mews
Rose Hill Cottages
Plunkett Court
St Laurence's College
Crawley's Court
Catherine's Steps
Strand Cottages
Ballast Quay
Paradise Place
Sienna Convent
Cord Road
St Catherine's Tce
Church (Presby)
Church Lane
William Street
St Laurence's Gate
Palace Row
Steam Packet Quay
Pumping Station
Monument
Marsh Road
Constitution Hill
St Laurence Street
Bachelors Lane
Merchant's Quay
Friary
Custom House
Custom House Quay
Ship Street
Augustinian Church
Bessexwell Lane
Mayoralty St
The Mall
De Lacy Bridge
South Quay
North Quay
Shop Street
St Mary's Bridge
Scotch Hall
Dublin Gate
Carmelite Cottages
Weirhope
Drogheda Main Drainage and Waste Disposal Scheme
osi
1
2
3

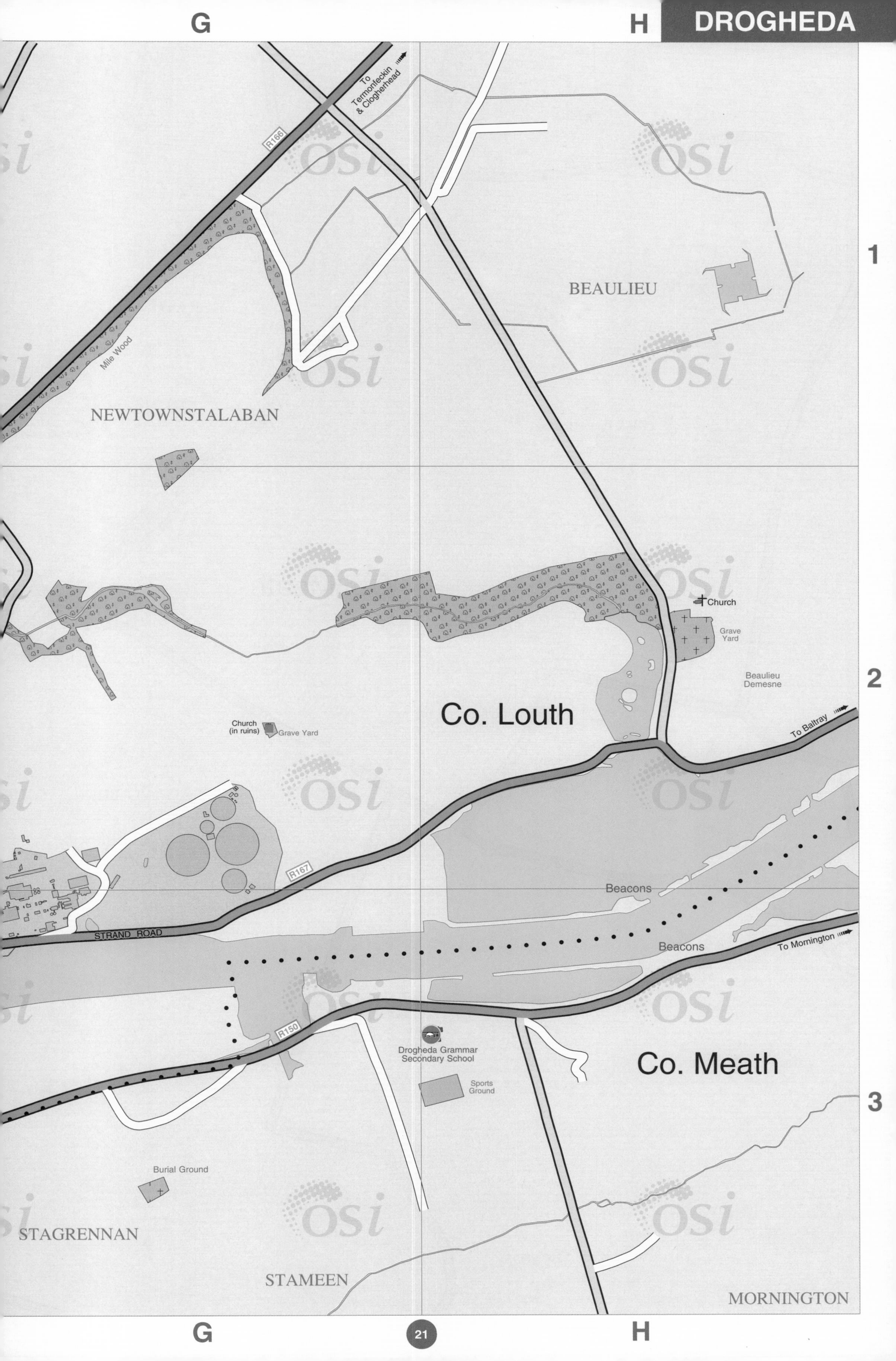
G
H
To Termonfeckin & Clogherhead
R166
Mile Wood
NEWTOWNSTALABAN
BEAULIEU
1
Church
Grave Yard
Beaulieu Demesne
2
Co. Louth
To Baltray
Church (in ruins)
Grave Yard
R167
Beacons
STRAND ROAD
Beacons
To Mornington
R150
Drogheda Grammar Secondary School
Co. Meath
Sports Ground
3
Burial Ground
STAGRENNAN
STAMEEN
MORNINGTON
G
H

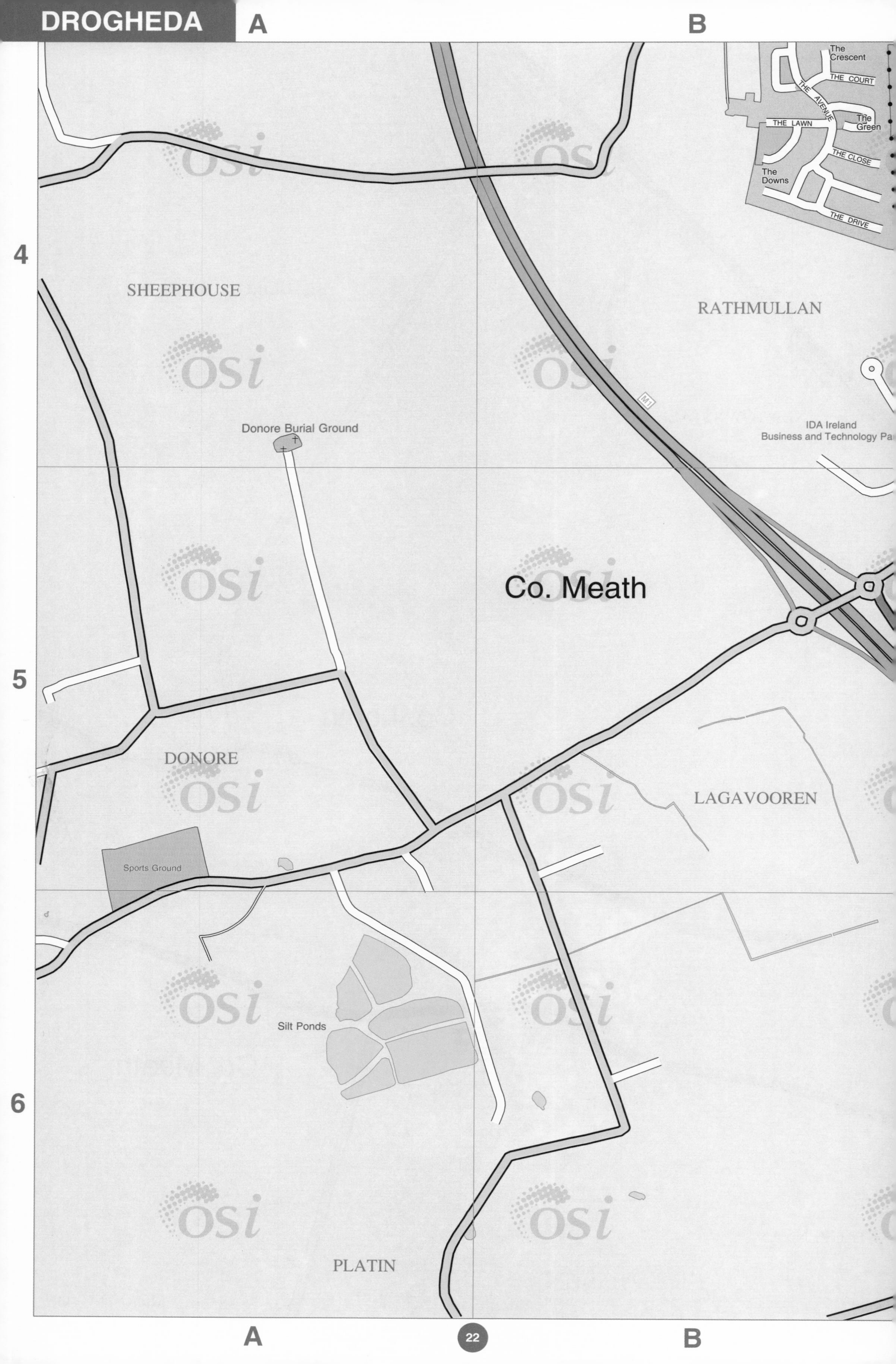
A
B
4
5
6
The Crescent
THE COURT
THE AVENUE
The Green
THE LAWN
THE CLOSE
The Downs
THE DRIVE
SHEEPHOUSE
RATHMULLAN
M1
Donore Burial Ground
IDA Ireland
Business and Technology Pa
Co. Meath
DONORE
LAGAVOOREN
Sports Ground
Silt Ponds
PLATIN
osi
A
B

C
D
Jim Pentony Park
Sports Ground
Sports Ground
Sports Ground
Rathmullan Park
Holy Family Boxing Club
Holy Family Church
Bus Station
Haymarket
Butter Gate
Highfield
Ballsgrove Health Centre
Marymount Primary School
Tredagh Close
Tredagh View
St Paul & St John's National Schools
MARLEY'S LANE
BEECHWOOD DRIVE
Ballsgrove Estate
St Finian's Park
Laurel Court
DONORE AVE
DONORE ROAD
Watery Hill
Mount St Oliver
School
Duleek Gate
AVENUE
PRIEST'S LANE
Corporation Cottages
Bottle Lane
Cherrybrook Drive
Hillbrook Drive
CONGRESS
PLATIN ROAD
4
Cherrymount
Marian Court
Marian Park
Moran's Terrace
Halpin's Terrace
Silk Park
Marley Court
Cedarfield Close
Cedarwood
Cedarfield
DONORE ROAD
P
Industrial Estate
Sports Ground
Elmwood
Oak Drive
Duleek Gate Bridge
McEVOY'S LANE
PLATIN ROAD
MATTHEW'S LANE
Wolfe Tones GAA Club
Newgrange Business Park
Donore Industrial Estate
Co. Meath
Drogheda Retail Park
Lagavooren Manor
Rathmullan Farm Bridge
Knockbrack Downs
5
R152
M1
BRYANSTOWN
6
To Duleek
To Dublin
C
D

E
F
Co. Louth
NEWTOWN
Co. Meath
BEY BEG
4
5
6
James Street
Barrack Street
Bull Ring
St Mary's Church (Cath)
Old Corn Market Hill
Fatima Mercy Convent School
Boyneview House
Pine Hamlet
Dublin Road
Poorhouse Lane
Presbytery
Sacred Heart Secondary School
St Mary's Hospital
St Mary's Villas
McBride Station
Newtown Bridge
Sampsons Lane
Corry's Hill
St Marys Court
Mary Street
Sunnyside Cottages
The Dale
Millmount Square
Dale Walk
Duleek Street
Cromwell's Lane
Cromwell's Mount
Railway Tce
Mc Grath's Lane
Fox Hill
Harvest Way
Acorn Way
Weaver's Way
Shady Grove
St Mary's Church (C of I)
St Mary's Cottages
Sports Ground
Legavooreen Park
Avondale
Autumn Way
Barley Cove
Coolagh Lodge (Appts)
St Patricks Cottages
Monastery
Rockville
Bryanstown Close
Mount Auburn
Wheaton Hall
Woodford
Leafy Haven
Copper Close
Sunhill
Blackbush Bridge
Bryanstown Manor
Ashdale
Woodgrove
St Mary's School
Clinton's Lane
Green View Cottages
Coolagh Well (Appts)
Collagh Court
Blackbush Lane
Cemetery
Bryanstown Court
R150
Oaten Vale
Bryanstown Village
Woodlane
The Park
Westwood
Longwood
Martello Village
Woodview
Cooley Bridge
Tunnel
Beymore Road
Meadow View
Beaubec
Beechmount Avenue
Rosevale
Blackbush Avenue
The Cairns
Forest
Area Under Development
Hazel Lane
Sports Ground
The Green
Five Oaks
Beamore Business Centre
The Park
The Drive
The Oaks
Millmount Abbey
Club House
Sports Ground
Five Oaks Village
Ard Rí
The Close
The Crescent
The Avenue
The View
R108
Motte
To Naul

Co. Meath
Dublin - Belfast Railway Line
COLP WEST
COLP EAST
PILLTOWN
KILTROUGH
PAINESTOWN
Colpa Fort (Site of)
Castle (Site of)
Grave Yard
St. Columba's Church
Monastery (Site of)
Forest View
Cairnes Court
Castlewood
STAMEEN LAWNS
MELROSE AVENUE
Stameen
SILVERSTREAM AVENUE
Area Under Development
The Boulevard
Park Lane
Park Crescent
Park Wood
Park Hill
Park Square
PARK WAY
Park Row
Park View
Park Close
PARK COURT
Park Green
PARK LAWN
PARK AVENUE
PARK DRIVE
Grange Rath
DUBLIN ROAD
R150
Woodgrange
To Julianstown
4
5
6

A
B
1
2
3
Blackhill Crescent
To Drogheda
Castle (site of)
Castle Glen
MORNINGTON CLOSE
BUTTERGATE WAY
ST LAURENCE'S ROAD
Mellifont Court
MANOR
JOHNSTON VILLAS
MORNINGTON AVE
MORNINGTON
DUKES COURT
DUKES VILLAS
Mornington Park
Donacarney National School
BETTYSTOWN ROAD
DONACARNEY GREAT
COLP EAST
R150
Area under Construction
BETAGHSTOW
Castlemartin Green
Wellesley Manor
Sevitt Manor
THE DRIVE
THE AVENUE
Sevitt Hall
THE GROVE
THE CLOSE
THE DALE
THE LAWN
THE GREEN
THE WALK
NARROWAY ROAD
THE CRESCENT
THE COURT
THE PARK
Draycott Lodge
Eastbury
Woodsi
Dublin/Belfast Railway
St.Colmcille's GFC
Cemetery
Club House
SEVITSLAND
BALLYMAD
MINISTOV
osi

INDEX

Bay View D2
Beach Park D3
Betaghstown Wood C2
Bettystown Road A1
Blackhill Crescent A1
Brabazon Bay C2
Brabazon Drive C1
Brabazon Green C1
Brabazon Links C1
Brookside C2
Burrow Cottages C2
Buttergate Way A1
Castle Glen A1
Castlemartin Green B1
Castlemartin Park C1
Donacarney A1
Draycott Lodge B2
Dukes Court A1
Dukes Villas A1
Eastbury B2
Eastham Court C2
Eastham Cove C2
Eastham Road C2
Eastham Village C2
Fairways Lawns C1
Fairways Park C1
Foxbury C1
Golf Links Road C1
Highfield D3
Inse Bay C3
Johnston Villas A1
Laytown C3
Mellifont Court A1
Mornington Avenue A1
Mornington Close A1
Mornington Manor A1
Mornington Park A1
Narroway Road B2
Neptune Terrace D2
Northlands C2
Seaview Terrace D2
Sevitt Hall B2
Sevitt Manor B2
St. Lawerences Road A1
St. Patrick's Square D3
St. Patrick's Villas D3
Strandview Terrace D2
The Anchorage C2
The Avenue, Sevitt Manor B2
The Bawn C2
The Cloisters C2
The Close, Inse Bay D3
The Close, Sevitt Hall B2
The Court, Sevitt Hall B2
The Crescent, Sevitt Hall B2
The Dale, Inse Bay D3
The Dale, Sevitt Manor B2
The Drive, Sevitt Manor B2
The Glade, Inse Bay C3
The Green, Inse Bay C3
The Green, Sevitt Manor B2
The Green, Woodside B2
The Grove, Sevitt Hall B2
The Lawn, Sevitt Hall B2
The Lawn, Inse Bay D3
The Maples C2
The Park, Sevitt Hall B2
The Terrace D3
The View, Woodside B2
The Walk, Sevitt Manor C3
The Wood, Inse Bay C3
Wellesley Manor B1
Woodside B2

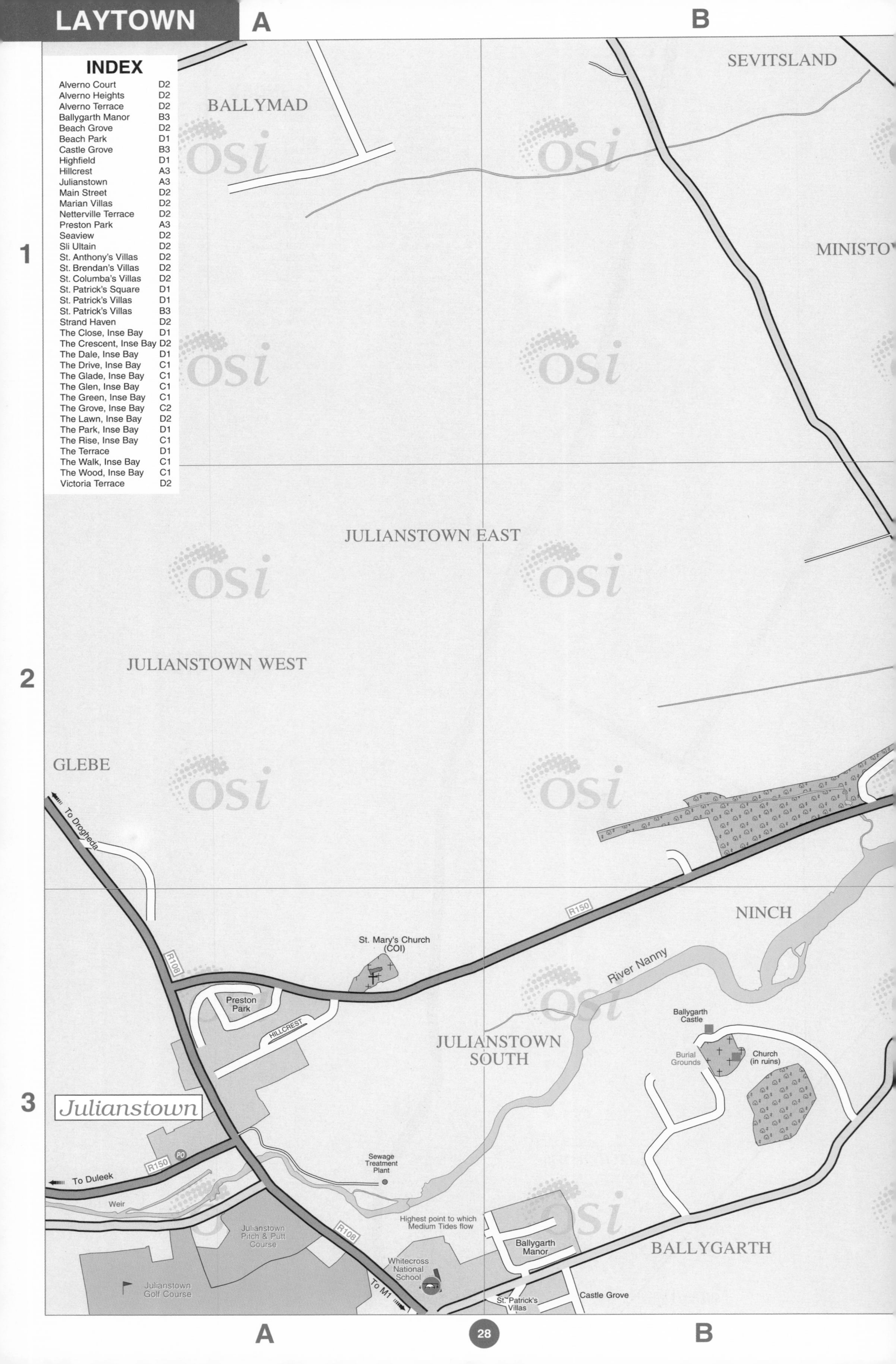
A
B
INDEX
Alverno Court D2
Alverno Heights D2
Alverno Terrace D2
Ballygarth Manor B3
Beach Grove D2
Beach Park D1
Castle Grove B3
Highfield D1
Hillcrest A3
Julianstown A3
Main Street D2
Marian Villas D2
Netterville Terrace D2
Preston Park A3
Seaview D2
Sli Ultain D2
St. Anthony's Villas D2
St. Brendan's Villas D2
St. Columba's Villas D2
St. Patrick's Square D1
St. Patrick's Villas D1
St. Patrick's Villas B3
Strand Haven D2
The Close, Inse Bay D1
The Crescent, Inse Bay D2
The Dale, Inse Bay D1
The Drive, Inse Bay C1
The Glade, Inse Bay C1
The Glen, Inse Bay C1
The Green, Inse Bay C1
The Grove, Inse Bay C2
The Lawn, Inse Bay D2
The Park, Inse Bay D1
The Rise, Inse Bay C1
The Terrace D1
The Walk, Inse Bay C1
The Wood, Inse Bay C1
Victoria Terrace D2
BALLYMAD
SEVITSLAND
MINISTO
1
JULIANSTOWN EAST
JULIANSTOWN WEST
2
GLEBE
To Drogheda
R150
NINCH
R108
St. Mary's Church (COI)
River Nanny
Preston Park
HILLCREST
Ballygarth Castle
JULIANSTOWN SOUTH
Burial Grounds
Church (in ruins)
3
Julianstown
PO
R150
To Duleek
Sewage Treatment Plant
Weir
Highest point to which Medium Tides flow
R108
Julianstown Pitch & Putt Course
Ballygarth Manor
BALLYGARTH
Whitecross National School
Julianstown Golf Course
To M1
St. Patrick's Villas
Castle Grove
A
B

C
D
St. Columbcille's Well (site of)
To Bettystown
R150
Scoil An Spioraid Naomh (Nat)
Saint Mary's Catholic Church
Beach Park
The Terrace
Highfield
St Patrick's Square
St Patrick's Villas
THE GLEN
THE DRIVE
THE WOOD
THE GLADE
THE PARK
THE GREEN
THE WALK
THE RISE
THE DALE
THE LAWN
THE CLOSE
NINCH
Inse Bay
The Crescent
The Grove
Sli Ultain
VICTORIA TERRACE
Netterville Terrace
ST ANTHONY'S VILLAS
ST COLUMBA'S VILLAS
Seaview
ST BENAN'S VILLAS
Alverno Court
Marian Villas
SEAMOUNT CRESCENT
Nursing Home
Alverno Heights
Strand Haven
Beach Grove
Laytown Railway Station
Dublin/Belfast Railway
ALVERNO TERRACE
MAIN ST
PO
P
IRISH SEA
Sonairte National Ecology Centre
Foot Bridge
Sewage Farm
River Nanny
Viaduct
Sports Ground
CORBALLIS
1
2
3

INDEX

Archdeaconry Glebe B1
Archdeaconry View A1
Ard Ná Gréine A1
Balrath Road A2
Balrath Wood A2
Bective Place B3
Bective Street A2
Beech Lawn B3
Blackthorn Close B1
Blackthorn Grove B1
Blackwater Heights A1
Cannon Street A2
Carraig Dun A1
Carrick Court A1
Carrick Street B1
Castle Street B2
Cavan Road A1
Cherry Hill Avenue A1
Cherry Hill Court B1
Cherry Hill Green B1
Cherry Hill Grove B1
Cherry Hill Road B1
Church Hill A2
Church Lane A2
Church Street B2
Circular Road A2
Climber Hall A2
Colmcille's Villas A1
Cross Carrick A2
Cross Street B2
Elm Grove B3
Fair Green A2
Farrell Street B2
Fr. McCullen Park A1
Gardenrath Close B3
Gardenrath Rd. Lr. B2
Gardenrath Rd. Upr. B3
Gooseberry Lane B1
Grand Priory B2
Headfort Glebe B2
Headfort Grove B1
Headfort Place B2
Headfort Road B2
Headfort Woods B1
Headfort Park B2
Hermitage Glen B2
John Street B2
Kenlis Crescent B2
Kenlis Place B2
Leather Alley B2
Lord Edward Street A1
Magdelene Court B1
Maple Drive B3
Market Street B2
Maudlin Court B1
Maudlin Street B1
Mill Lane B1
Moy Place B1
Moynalty Road A1
Navan Road B2
New Market Street B2
Newrath View A2
O'Growney Terrace A1
Oliver Plunket Road A1
Park Lodge A2
Pitcher Lane B1
Rochford Hall A1
Rockfield Road A2
St. Bridgid's Terrace A1
St. Patrick's Terrace B1
Stonebridge B1
Suffolk Street A2
Sunset Heights A1
Sycamore Avenue B3
Taylor Hall A1
Termon Hall B2
The Cloisters A1
The Glebe B1
The Grove B2
The Orchard B2
Tiermurrin Lane A3
Tober Bán A2
Willie Black Crescent B1

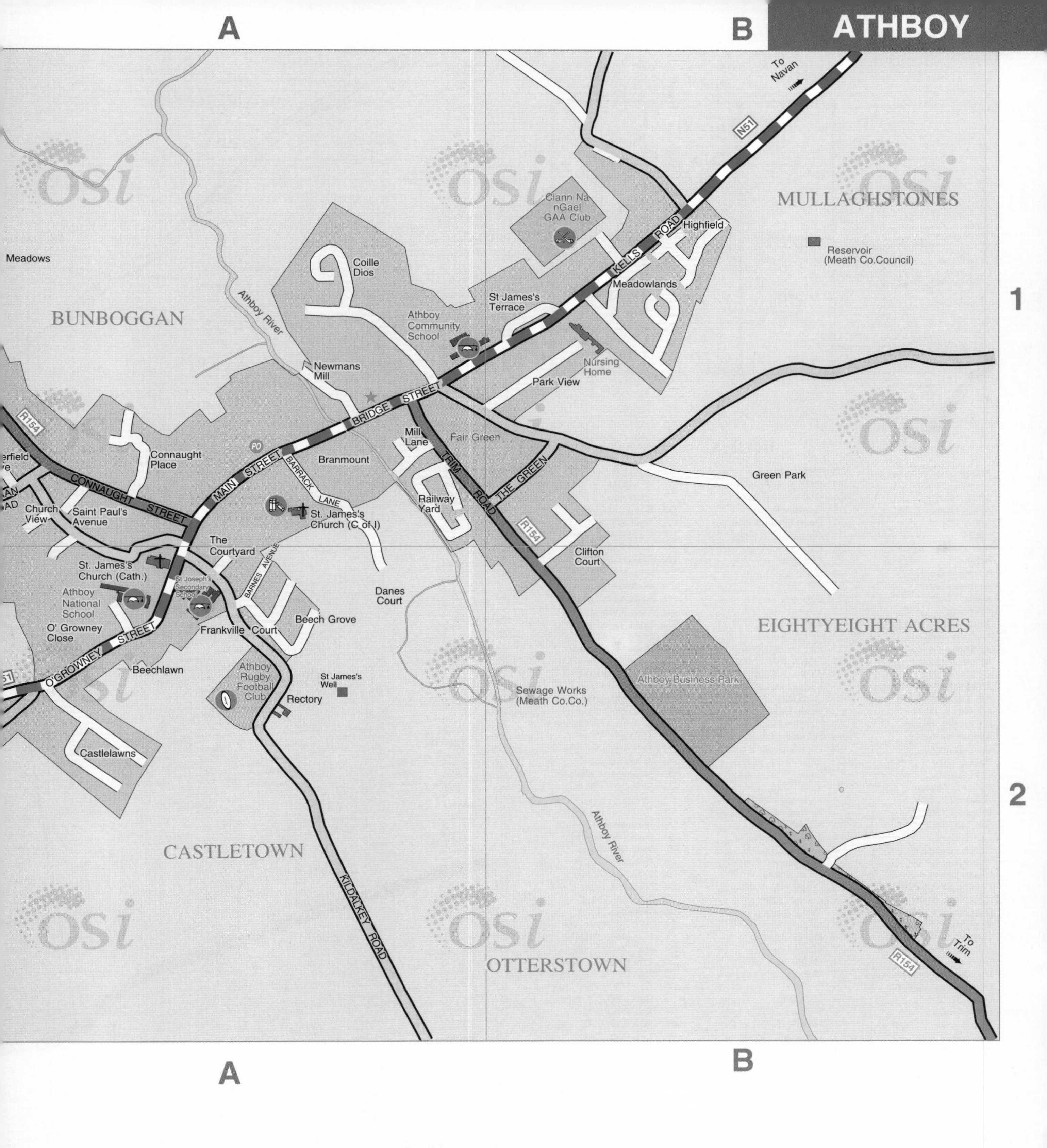

INDEX

Athboy Business Park	B2	Highfield	B1
Barnes Avenue	A2	Kells Road	B1
Barrack Lane	A2	Kildalkey Road	A2
Beech Grove	A2	Main Street	A1
Beechlawn	A2	Meadowlands	B1
Branmount	A1	Mill Lane	A1
Bridge Street	A1	Newmans Mill	A1
Butterfield Grove	A1	O'Growney Close	A2
Castle Avenue	B1	O'Growney Street	A2
Castlelawns	A2	Park View	B1
Church View	A1	Railway Yard	A1
Clifton Court	B2	St. James's Terrace	B1
Cloran Court	A1	St. Joseph's Villas	A1
Cloran Road	A1	St. Paul's Avenue	A1
Coille Dios	A1	The Courtyard	B2
Connaught Place	A1	The Green	B1
Connaught Street	A1	The Rise	A1
Danes Court	A2	Trim Road	A1
Frankville Court	A2	Turry Meadows	A1
Green Park	B1		

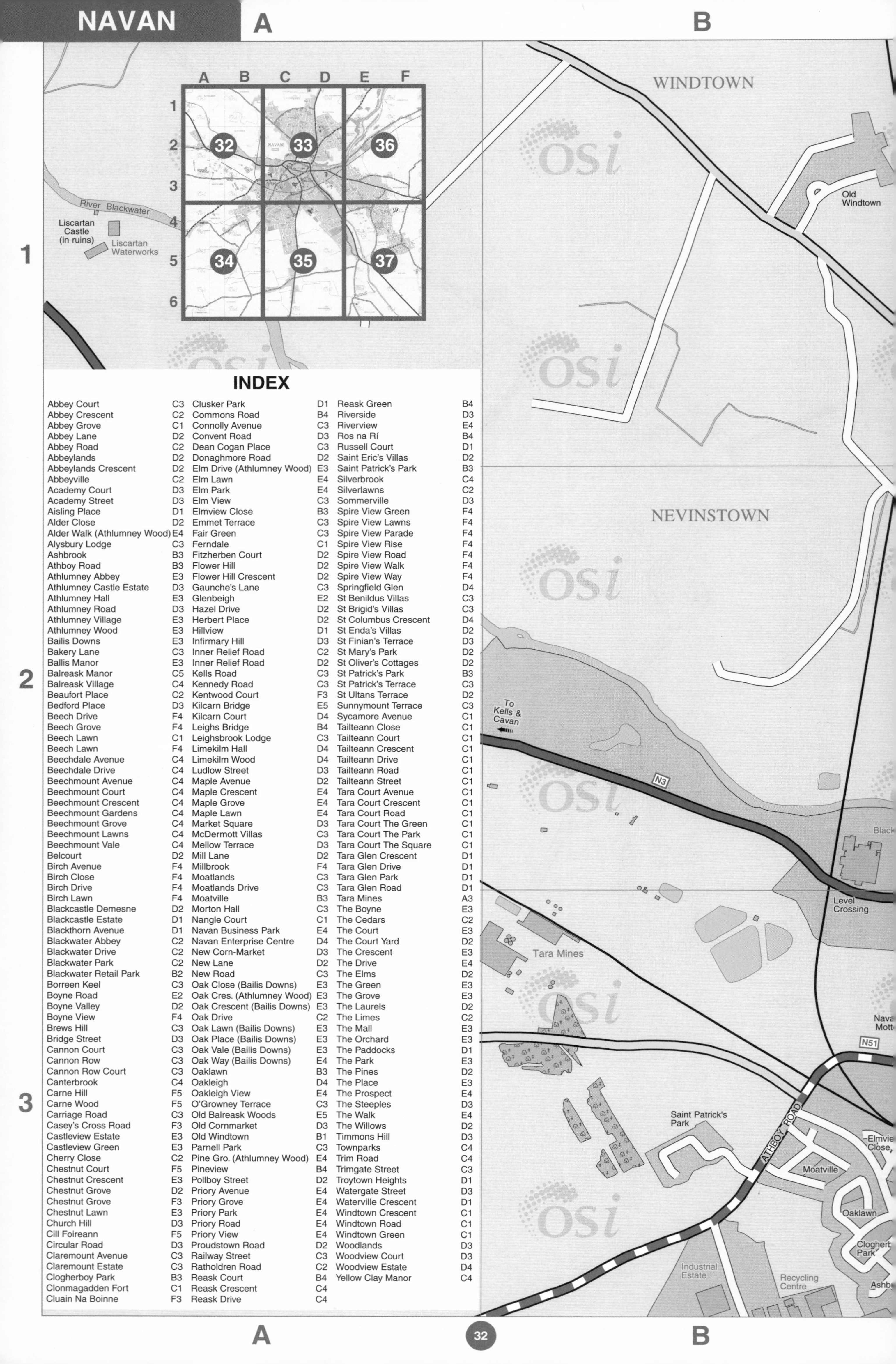

INDEX

Abbey Court C3
Abbey Crescent C2
Abbey Grove C1
Abbey Lane D2
Abbey Road C2
Abbeylands D2
Abbeylands Crescent D2
Abbeyville C2
Academy Court D3
Academy Street D3
Aisling Place D1
Alder Close D2
Alder Walk (Athlumney Wood) E4
Alysbury Lodge C3
Ashbrook B3
Athboy Road B3
Athlumney Abbey E3
Athlumney Castle Estate D3
Athlumney Hall E3
Athlumney Road D3
Athlumney Village E3
Athlumney Wood E3
Bailis Downs E3
Bakery Lane C3
Ballis Manor E3
Balreask Manor C5
Balreask Village C4
Beaufort Place C2
Bedford Place D3
Beech Drive F4
Beech Grove F4
Beech Lawn C1
Beech Lawn F4
Beechdale Avenue C4
Beechdale Drive C4
Beechmount Avenue C4
Beechmount Court C4
Beechmount Crescent C4
Beechmount Gardens C4
Beechmount Grove C4
Beechmount Lawns C4
Beechmount Vale C4
Belcourt D2
Birch Avenue F4
Birch Close F4
Birch Drive F4
Birch Lawn F4
Blackcastle Demesne D2
Blackcastle Estate D1
Blackthorn Avenue D1
Blackwater Abbey C2
Blackwater Drive C2
Blackwater Park C2
Blackwater Retail Park B2
Borreen Keel C3
Boyne Road E2
Boyne Valley D2
Boyne View F4
Brews Hill C3
Bridge Street D3
Cannon Court C3
Cannon Row C3
Cannon Row Court C3
Canterbrook C4
Carne Hill F5
Carne Wood F5
Carriage Road C3
Casey's Cross Road F3
Castleview Estate E3
Castleview Green E3
Cherry Close C2
Chestnut Court F5
Chestnut Crescent E3
Chestnut Grove D2
Chestnut Grove F3
Chestnut Lawn E3
Church Hill D3
Cill Foireann F5
Circular Road D3
Claremount Avenue C3
Claremount Estate C3
Clogherboy Park B3
Clonmagadden Fort C1
Cluain Na Boinne F3
Clusker Park D1
Commons Road B4
Connolly Avenue C3
Convent Road D3
Dean Cogan Place C3
Donaghmore Road D2
Elm Drive (Athlumney Wood) E3
Elm Lawn E4
Elm Park E4
Elm View C3
Elmview Close B3
Emmet Terrace C3
Fair Green C3
Ferndale C1
Fitzherben Court D2
Flower Hill D2
Flower Hill Crescent D2
Gaunche's Lane C3
Glenbeigh E2
Hazel Drive D2
Herbert Place D2
Hillview D1
Infirmary Hill D3
Inner Relief Road C2
Inner Relief Road D2
Kells Road C3
Kennedy Road C3
Kentwood Court F3
Kilcarn Bridge E5
Kilcarn Court D4
Leighs Bridge B4
Leighsbrook Lodge C3
Limekilm Hall D4
Limekilm Wood D4
Ludlow Street D3
Maple Avenue D2
Maple Crescent E4
Maple Grove E4
Maple Lawn E4
Market Square D3
McDermott Villas C3
Mellow Terrace D3
Mill Lane D2
Millbrook F4
Moatlands C3
Moatlands Drive C3
Moatville B3
Morton Hall C3
Nangle Court C1
Navan Business Park E4
Navan Enterprise Centre D4
New Corn-Market D3
New Lane D2
New Road C3
Oak Close (Bailis Downs) E3
Oak Cres. (Athlumney Wood) E3
Oak Crescent (Bailis Downs) E3
Oak Drive C2
Oak Lawn (Bailis Downs) E3
Oak Place (Bailis Downs) E3
Oak Vale (Bailis Downs) E3
Oak Way (Bailis Downs) E4
Oaklawn B3
Oakleigh D4
Oakleigh View E4
O'Growney Terrace C3
Old Balreask Woods E5
Old Cornmarket D3
Old Windtown B1
Parnell Park C3
Pine Gro. (Athlumney Wood) E4
Pineview B4
Pollboy Street D2
Priory Avenue E4
Priory Grove E4
Priory Park E4
Priory Road E4
Priory View E4
Proudstown Road D2
Railway Street C3
Ratholdren Road C2
Reask Court B4
Reask Crescent C4
Reask Drive C4
Reask Green B4
Riverside D3
Riverview E4
Ros na Rí B4
Russell Court D1
Saint Eric's Villas D2
Saint Patrick's Park B3
Silverbrook C4
Silverlawns C2
Sommerville D3
Spire View Green F4
Spire View Lawns F4
Spire View Parade F4
Spire View Rise F4
Spire View Road F4
Spire View Walk F4
Spire View Way F4
Springfield Glen D4
St Benildus Villas C3
St Brigid's Villas C3
St Columbus Crescent D4
St Enda's Villas D2
St Finian's Terrace D3
St Mary's Park D2
St Oliver's Cottages D2
St Patrick's Park B3
St Patrick's Terrace C3
St Ultans Terrace D2
Sunnymount Terrace C3
Sycamore Avenue C1
Tailteann Close C1
Tailteann Court C1
Tailteann Crescent C1
Tailteann Drive C1
Tailteann Road C1
Tailteann Street C1
Tara Court Avenue C1
Tara Court Crescent C1
Tara Court Road C1
Tara Court The Green C1
Tara Court The Park C1
Tara Court The Square C1
Tara Glen Crescent D1
Tara Glen Drive D1
Tara Glen Park D1
Tara Glen Road D1
Tara Mines A3
The Boyne E3
The Cedars C2
The Court E3
The Court Yard D2
The Crescent E3
The Drive E4
The Elms D2
The Green E3
The Grove E3
The Laurels D2
The Limes C2
The Mall E3
The Orchard E3
The Paddocks D1
The Park E3
The Pines D2
The Place E3
The Prospect E4
The Steeples D3
The Walk E4
The Willows D2
Timmons Hill D3
Townparks C4
Trim Road C4
Trimgate Street C3
Troytown Heights D1
Watergate Street D3
Waterville Crescent D1
Windtown Crescent C1
Windtown Road C1
Windtown Green C1
Woodlands D3
Woodview Court D3
Woodview Estate D4
Yellow Clay Manor C4

C
D
1
2
3
CLONMAGADDAN
BATTERSTOWN
BLACKCASTLE
Simonstown GAA
WINDTOWN ROAD
To Kingscourt
R162
The Paddocks
Tailteann Crescent
Tailteann Court
Tara Glen Estate
Crescent
The Square
Tara Court Estate
The Green
Area Under Construction
Windtown Green
Navan Leisure Centre
Windtown Crescent
Clonmagadden Fort
Nangle Court
Troytown Heights
Hillview
Clusker Park
Blackcastle Estate
Abbey Grove
Ferndale
Blackthorn Avenue
Russell Court
Sycamore Avenue
Beech Lawn
Beaufort Place
St. Oliver Plunkett's Church
St. Oliver's Cottages
Belcourt
Boyne Valley
Cherry Close
Oak Drive
The Laurels
The Pines
The Willows
Maple Avenue
The Cedar's
Alder Close
Hazel Drive
The Limes
St. Mary's Park
Saint Eric's Villas
DONAGHMORE ROAD
N51
Blackcastle Demesne
Blackwater Abbey
Chestnut Grove
Sports Ground
St. Enda's Villas
Fitzherbert Court
Silverlawns
St. Paul's Primary School
INNER RELIEF ROAD
Abbey Crescent
Abbeylands Crescent
St. Ultan's School
The Court Yard
Herbert Place
Blackwater Mill
Flower Hill Crescent
River Blackwater
Industrial Estate
V.E.C.
St. Ultan's Terrace
Abbey Court
Town Hall
Pollboy Bridge
River Boyne
Ruxton Lock
BOYNE ROAD
Scoil Mhuire
Navan
Dean Cogan Place
O' Growney Terrace
KENNEDY ROAD
New Bridge
ATHLUMNEY ROAD
R153
Sommerville
Loreto Convent Secondary School (St. Michael's)
MARKET SQUARE
The Steeples
Alysbury Lodge
Canon Row Court
Emmet Terrace
Cannon Court
TRIMGATE STREET
St. Anne's Resource Centre
St. Mary's Church (C of I)
New Corn-Market
Church Hill
Bedford Place
Infirmary Hill
Infirmary
MOATLANDS
Sunnymount Terrace
BREWS HILL
Morton Hall
CIRCULAR ROAD
Athlumney Bridge
Riverside
Grave Yard
Athlumney Castle (In Ruins)
St. Joseph's Mercy Primary & Secondary Schools
Scoil Aine Naofa
St Finian's Terrace
Co.Co. Offices
County Hall
Navan Station
Athlumney Castle Estate
St. Mary's Convent Of Mercy
Navan Hospital
Pairc Tailteann
Leighsbrook Lodge
H.S.E.
St Benildus Villas
Swimming Pool
L.C.
McDermott Villas
Abylity Education Centre
CARRIAGE ROAD
Woodlands
Mellow Terrace
Academy Court
ACADEMY STREET
Parnell Park
Connolly Avenue
Nursing Home
Claremont Estate
Claremount Avenue
Pitch & Putt Club
NEW ROAD
Flowerfield National School
Woodview Court

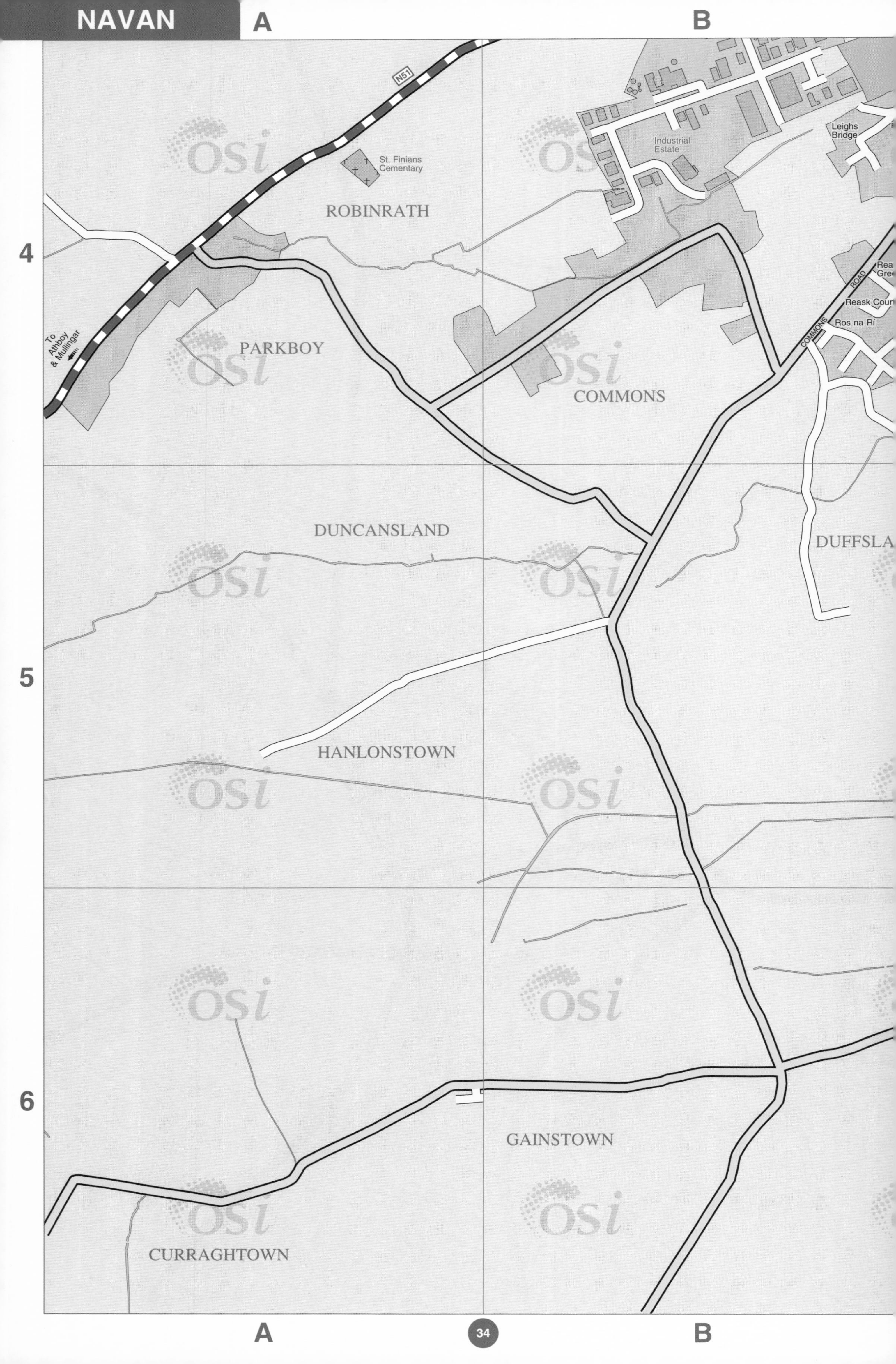
A
B
N51
St. Finians
Cementary
ROBINRATH
To
Athboy
& Mullingar
PARKBOY
Industrial
Estate
Leighs
Bridge
COMMONS ROAD
Reask Court
Ros na Rí
COMMONS
DUFFSLA
DUNCANSLAND
HANLONSTOWN
GAINSTOWN
CURRAGHTOWN
4
5
6
A
B

C
D
Day Care Centre
Yellow Clay Manor
Beechmount Industrial Estate
Beechmount Vale
GARDENS
COURT
BEECHDALE DR
AVENUE
BEECHDALE
GROVE
Beechmount
CRESCENT
AVENUE
BEECHMOUNT
Beechmount Lawns
Townparks
Balreask Village
Silverbrook
Reask Crescent
Canterbrook
Balreask Manor
TRIM ROAD
R161
Oil Depot
Navan Enterprise Centre
Woodview Estate
St Columbus Crescent
Scoil Eanna
Beaufort College Secondary School
Limekiln Wood
Sports Ground
Monument
Limekiln Hall
Springfield Glen
Kilcarn Court
Navan R.F.C.
Club House
Oakleigh
BALREASK OLD
PHILPOTSTOWN
KENNASTOWN
To Trim
4
5
6

E
F
To Slane Drogheda & M1
Church (in ruins)
Round Tower
Grave Yard
N51
Rowley's Lock
Sewage Treatment Plant
ARDMULCHAN
1
Fish Weir
River Boyne
Canal (Disused)
Salmon Hatchery
BLACKCASTLE DEMESNE
Area Under Development
BOYNE ROAD
Glenbeigh
The Rampart
2
Cemetery
FERGANSTOWN and BALLYMACON
Salmon Trap
Bailis Manor
Castleview Green
The Grove
Castleview Estate
The Orchard
3
Athlumney Village
ALEXANDER REID
R153
The Green
THE COURT
Athlumney Abbey
Athlumney Hall
Kentwood Court
Oak Vale
Oak Close
Athlumney Wood
Cluain Na Boinne
The Boyne
The Park
THE PLACE
The Crescent
THE MALL
ELM DRIVE
Oak Crescent
Oak Place
Lawn
Oak Crescent
Bailis Downs
Chestnut Lawn
Chestnut Crescent
Chestnut Grove
BAILIS
To Drogheda
E
F

THE WALK
The Park
The Drive
Pine Grove
Oak Way
Oak
Athlumney Abbey
Alder Walk
The Prospect
Riverview
Johnstown Centre
The Bailis Resource Centre
ATHLUMNEY
Elm Lawn
Elm Park
Birch Drive
Birch Close
Birch Avenue
Birch Lawn
St. Stephen's National School
St.Martha's College
Maple Crescent
Maple Grove
Maple Lawn
Beech Drive
Beech Lawn
Beech Grove
Priory Grove
Priory View
PRIORY ROAD
Priory Park
Priory Avenue
Millbrook
Navan Business and Technology Park
Boyne View
Lawns
PARADE
Walk
Spire View Estate
WAY
Green
SPIRE VIEW ROAD
RISE
Factory
Athlumney House
River Boyne
N3
JOHNSTOWN
Church Of The Assumption
Chestnut Court
Cill Foireann
Balreask Woods
Carne Wood
Carne Hill
St. Mary's School
Grave Yard
Weir
KILCARN
BOYNEHILL or BALLAGH
St. Brigid's National School
ARDSALLAGH
River Boyne
To Dunshaughlin & Dublin
A B C D E F
1 2 3 4 5 6
32 33 36 34 35 37

A
B
1
2
3
LONGFORD
NEWTOWN
High Meadows
Newtown Bridge
GOOSE TAIL AVENUE
LONGFORD ROAD
STATION ROAD
Kingshill
Ashvale Court
Kingsgate
Fr.Ryan Park
DOWNESTOWN
Larrix Court
Paramadda River
Stoneyford Green
Cill Carban
The Laurels
The Willows
LARRIX STREET
River View
The Hawthorns
Larrix Mews
Parish Centre
MAIN ST
Limetree Close
The Steeples
DAVIES LANE
Saint Cianan's Church
The County Co.Council Office
COLGAN STREET
St. Cianan's Church (In Ruins)
CHURCH LANE
Church
Casey's Lane
Oakl
TOWER VIEW AVENUE
St.Mary's Abbey (In Ruins)
Abbeyland
Club House
Duleek Court
Duleek GAA Club
NAVAN ROAD
Bathe Abbey
Wayside Cross
Balsaran Close
The Belfry
Ford
Balsaran Park
ABBEY ROAD
Abbey (in ruins)
To Kentstown & Navan
R150
St. Cianan's Villas
Duleek House
BALSARAN
ABBEYLAND
River Nanny
Duleek National School
R152
To N2 Ashbourne & Finglas
A
B

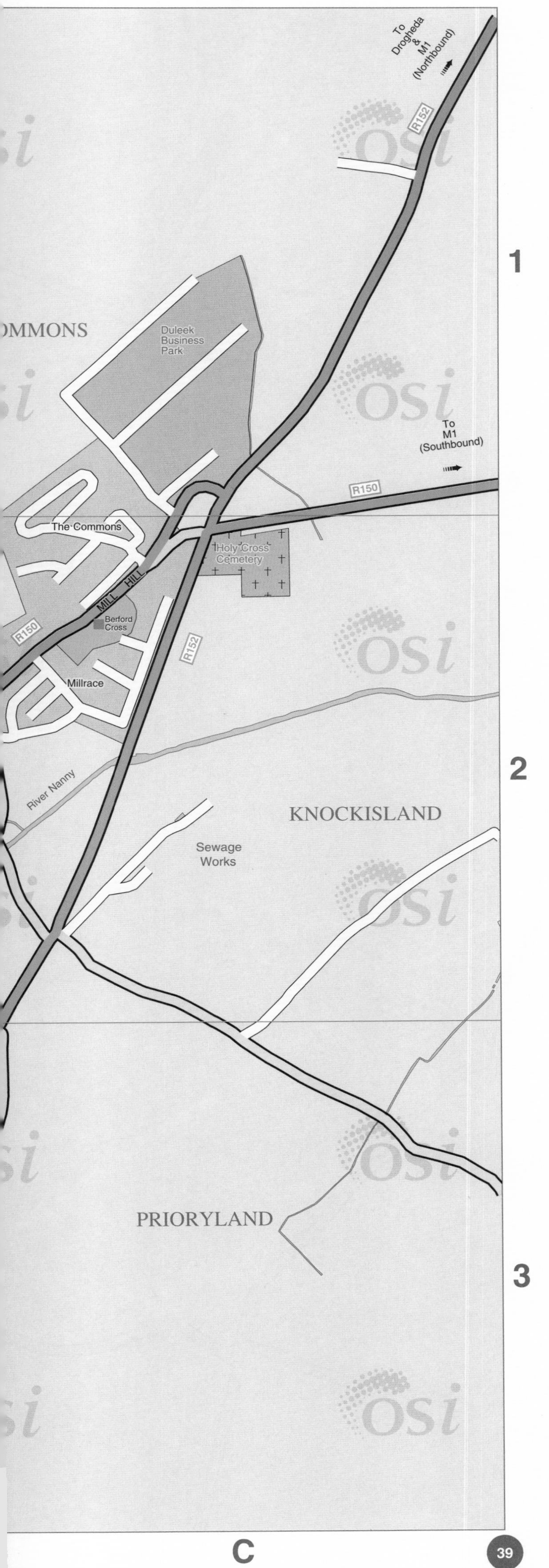

INDEX

Abbey Road B2
Abbeylands B2
Ashvale Court B2
Balsaran Close B2
Balsaran Park B2
Bathe Abbey B2
Casey's Lane B2
Church Lane B2
Cill Carban A2
Colgan Street B2
Davies Lane B2
Duleek Business Park C1
Duleek Court B2
Fr. Ryan Park B2
Goose Tail Avenue B1
High Meadows B1
Kingsgate B2
Kingshill B1
Larrix Court B2
Larrix Mews B2
Larrix Street B2
Limetree Close B2
Longford Road A1
Main Street B2
Mill Hill C2
Millrace C2
Navan Road B2
Newtown Bridge A1
Oakleigh B2
River View B2
St. Cianan's Villas B2
Station Road B1
Stoneyford Green B2
The Belfry A2
The Commons C2
The Courtyard B2
The Hawthorns A2
The Laurels A2
The Steeples B2
The Willows A2
Tower View Avenue A2

A
B
INDEX
Balscadden Road A2
Cock Hill Road A1
Delvin Centre Apts B2
Elvana A2
Forge Hill Close A2
Forge Hill Crescent A2
Forge Hill Drive A1
Forge Hill Green A1
Forge Hill Park A1
Forge Hill Way A1
Gormanstown Road B1
Gracemeadow Avenue A2
Gracemeadow Court A2
Gracemeadow Dale A2
Gracemeadow Grove A2
Gracemeadow Park A2
Gracemeadow Way A2
Lemare A2
Main Street A2
Mill Close A2
Mill Crescent A2
Mill Drive A2
Mill Green A2
Mill Lane A2
Mill Lawns A2
Mill Park A2
Mill Park A2
Mill View A2
Mill Road A2
Mill Way A2
Mountain View A2
Orchard Close A2
Orchard Drive A2
Orchard Rise A2
Orchard Vale A2
Orchard View A2
Silverstream Close A2
The Grange B1
Village Estate A2
Village Close A2
Village Drive A2
Village Green A2
Village Grove A2
Watery Lane A2
1
2
3
To Drogheda & Belfast
M1
The Grange
St. Patrick's GAA Club
Community Centre
GORMANSTOWN ROAD
Co. Meath
Under Construction
St. Patrick's School
COCK HILL ROAD
Forgehill Estate
Gormanstown Meadows
Delvin River
Gracemeadow Estate
Mill Estate
Orchard Estate
Village Estate
Sewage Works
Grave Yard
Church (In Ruins)
Lemare
Delvin Centre Apts.
St. Patrick's Catholic Church
Silverstream Close
Elvana
Mountain View
Stadalt Cross
MAIN STREET
Co. Dublin
STADALT
BALSCADDAN ROAD
To Balbriggan Swords M50 & Dublin
Stedalt House Nursing Home
MILESTOWN
SEVENPARKS
TOBERTOWN
A
B

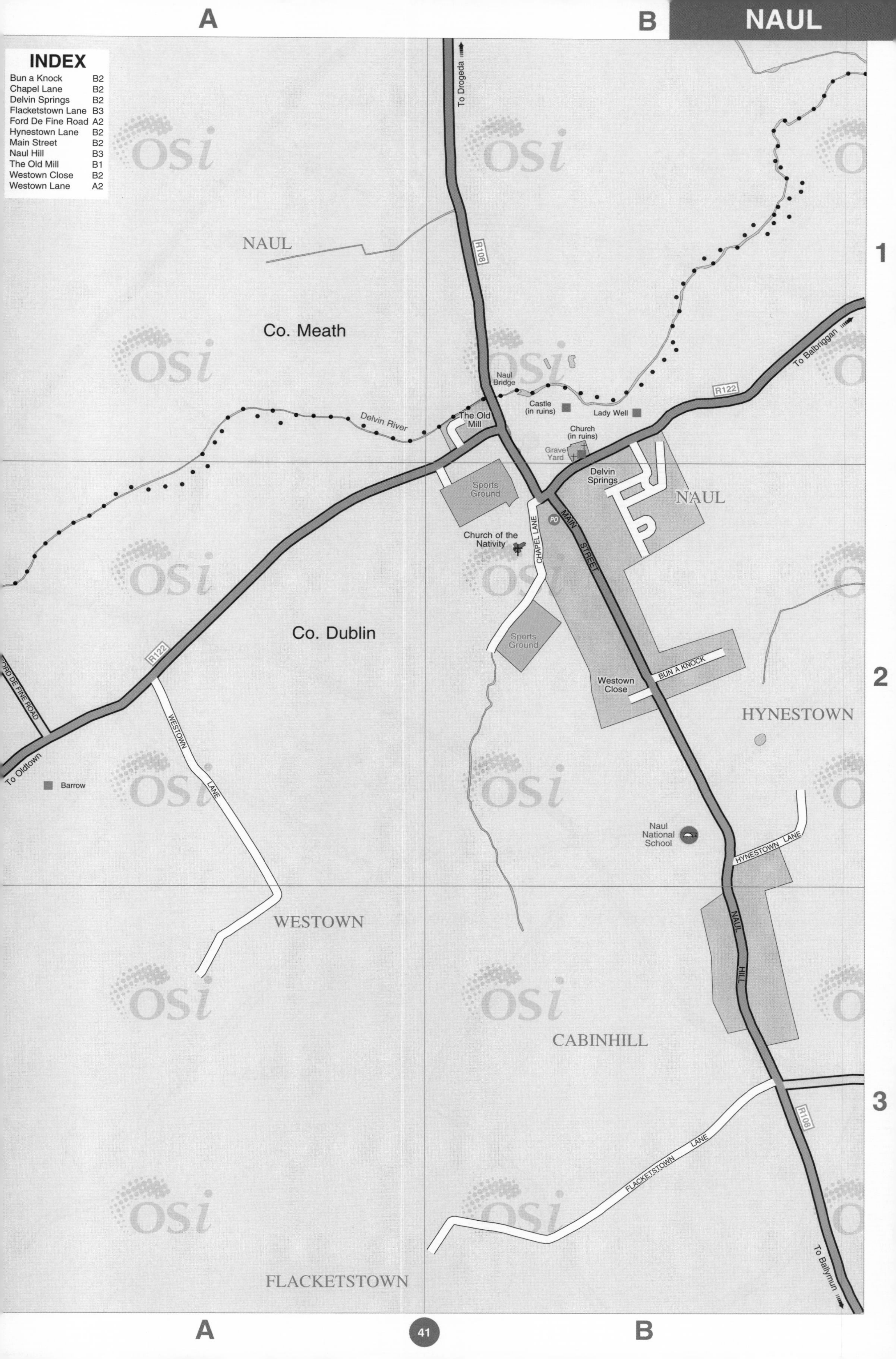
A
B
INDEX
Bun a Knock B2
Chapel Lane B2
Delvin Springs B2
Flacketstown Lane B3
Ford De Fine Road A2
Hynestown Lane B2
Main Street B2
Naul Hill B3
The Old Mill B1
Westown Close B2
Westown Lane A2
To Drogeda
R108
NAUL
Co. Meath
Naul Bridge
Castle (in ruins)
Lady Well
Delvin River
The Old Mill
Church (in ruins)
Grave Yard
To Balbriggan
R122
Sports Ground
Delvin Springs
NAUL
Church of the Nativity
CHAPEL LANE
MAIN STREET
PO
Co. Dublin
Sports Ground
BUN A KNOCK
Westown Close
FORD DE FINE ROAD
R122
WESTOWN LANE
HYNESTOWN
To Oldtown
Barrow
Naul National School
HYNESTOWN LANE
WESTOWN
NAUL HILL
CABINHILL
R108
FLACKETSTOWN LANE
To Ballymun
FLACKETSTOWN
1
2
3

A
B
1
2
3
To Drogheda
BREMORE
FLEMINGTOWN
Dublin/Belfast Railway
Sports Ground
R132
Cardy Rock
O'Dwyers GAA Club
Castle (in Ruins)
St Molaga's Church (in Ruins)
Saint Molaga's National School
Mount Rochford
Clonuske
New Haven
FLEMINGTON LANE
HAMLET LANE
DROGHEDA ROAD
Bremore Castle
Trimelston
Chieftain's Way
Ashfield
Lambeecher
Baron's Hall
Hampton Woods
Chapel Gate
CHIEFTAIN'S ROAD
MOYLARAGH ROAD
Balbriggan Community College
Moylaragh
Westbrook
Saint Peter and Paul's Junior School
St Peter and Paul's Cemetery
R122
CLONARD ROAD
CLOGHEDER
HARRY REYNOLDS ROAD
Balbriggan Park
Fingal Bay Business Park
Stephenstown Business Park
CLONARD or FOLKSTOWN GREAT
To M1 and Naul
STEPHENSTOWN
Halting Site
FOLKSTOWN LITTLE
M1

INDEX

Ardgillen Close C3
Ardgillen Drive C3
Ardgillen Heights C3
Ardgillen Lawn C3
Ardgillen Road C3
Ashfield Close B1
Ashfield Drive B1
Ashfield Green B1
Ashfield Rise B1
Ashfield Way B1
Balbriggan Business Park B2
Baron's Hall A1
Baron's Hall House A1
Baron's Hall Lodge A1
Baron's Hall The Grove A1
Baron's Hall The Rise A1
Baths Road B1
Baths Road C1
Bellsfield Court B1
Brecan Close B1
Brega B1
Bremore Castle B1
Bremore Court B1
Bremore Drive B1
Brick Lane C2
Bridge Street C2
Cardy Rock Avenue B1
Cardy Rock Close B1
Cardy Rock Court B1
Cardy Rock Crescent B1
Cardy Rock Road B1
Cardy Rock Square B1
Cardy Rock Walk B1
Castleland Court C3
Castlelands C3
Chapel Avenue B2
Chapel Close B2
Chapel Court C2
Chapel Gate B2
Chapel Grove B2
Chapel Street C2
Chapel Street Crescent C2
Chieftain's Close B1
Chieftain's Crescent B1
Chieftain's Drive B1
Chieftan's Road B1
Chieftain's Way B1
Clonard Court B2
Clonard Rise B2
Clonard Road A2
Clonard Street B2
Clonuske Close B1
Clonuske Drive B1
Clonuske Gardens B1
Clonuske Rise B1
Clonuske View B1
Convent Lane C2
Cornmill Apartments C2
Covetown B1
Craobhin Park C2
Curran Park C2
Derham Park D2
Dublin Street C2
Fancourt D2
Fancourt Heights D2
Fingal Bay Business Pk. B2
Flemington Lane A1
Flemington Park A1
Fullam Terrace B2
George's Court C2
George's Hill C2
George's Street C2
Gibbons Terrace C2
Glover Court C2
Hamlet Avenue A1
Hamlet Close B1
Hamlet Lane B1
Hamlet Lane House A1
Hampton Court C2
Hampton Cove D2
Hampton Green C2
Hampton Place C2
Hampton Street C2
Hampton Woods B1
Harbour Road C2
Harry Reynolds Road B2
High Street C2
Lambeecher B1
Laragh C2
Lawless Terrace C2
Linnen Hall C2[1]
Market Garden C2
Market Green C2
McWeill Hall C2[2]
Mill Race C2
Mill Street C2
Mill Walk C2
Mount Rochford B1
Mount Rochford Avenue B1
Mount Rochford Close B1
Mount Rochford Drive B1
Mount Rochford Park B1
Mount Rochford Rise B1
Moylaragh Avenue B2
Moylaragh Close B2
Moylaragh Court B2
Moylaragh Crescent B2
Moylaragh Drive B2
Moylaragh Gardens A2
Moylaragh Grove B2
Moylaragh Lane A2
Moylaragh Mews A2
Moylaragh Road B2
Moylaragh Walk B2
Moylaragh Way B2
New Haven Avenue B1
New Haven Bay B1
New Haven Close B1
New Haven Court B1
New Haven Park B1
New Haven Rise B1
Oakleigh B2
Papworth Hall C2[3]
Pine Ridge B2
Pinewood Green Avenue D3
Pinewood Green Close C3
Pinewood Green Court D3
Pinewood Green Hill D3
Pinewood Green Lawn C3
Pinewood Green Road D3
Pump Lane C2
Quay Street C2
Railway Street C2
Seapoint Lane C2
Skerries Road C2
St. Molagha's Terrace C2
St. Paul's Crescent C2
St. Peter's Terrace C2
Stephenstown Bus. Pk. B3
Tanners Water Lane C3
Tara Court B2
Tara Cove B2
Templeville B1
The Chantries C3
The Square C2
Trimelston A1
Vauxhall Street C2
Westbrook Avenue B2
Westbrook Close B2
Westbrook Crescent B2
Westbrook Drive B2
Westbrook Green B2
Westbrook Green B2
Westbrook Lawn B2
Westbrook Park B2
Westbrook Rise B2

Streets not named but shown as small numbers:

C2 1 Linnen Hall
2 McWeill Hall
3 Papworth Hall

A
B
1
2
3
R127
BALBRIGGAN ROAD
To Balbriggan
Kelly's Bay
VIEW
PIER
BEACH
COVE
STRAND
SHORE
ROCKS
INLET
MOORINGS
PROMENADE
THE PROMENADE
HEIGHTS
TOWER
DRIVE
WEIR
CLIFFS
WINDMILL DRIVE
WINDMILL COURT
WINDMILL CLOSE
AN CLADDAGH
ARDGILLAN VIEW
NORTHCLIFFE HEIGHTS
HARRISON'S COVE
Mourne View
MOURNE CLOSE
MOURNE DR
MOURNE COURT
MOURNE GROVE
MOURNE PARK
MOURNE PLACE
Area Under Construction
THE GREEN
THE HEIGHTS
THE RISE
THE WAY
THE LAWN
THE DRIVE
Skerries Rock
SELSKAR COURT
THE VALE
THE WALK
SELSKAR AVENUE
SELSKAR RD
SELSKAR RISE
SHALLOCH HILL GROVE
NEW
TOWNPARKS
THE BRAMBLES
TOWN PARKS
Scoil Realt na Mara
THE VIEW
THE PARK
THE GREEN
THE COURT
THE GROVE
THE CRES
AVENUE
SEA CREST
MOORING COVE
THE HOAR ROCK
BALBRIGGAN ROAD
NORTH STRAND
Holy Faith De La Salle College
THE PARK
FOX GROVE
TOWNSPARK
ARDLA
Sports Ground
ST. PATRICK'S CLOSE
STATION ROAD
Skerries Train Station
Tennis Ground
DUBLIN
Ardla Burial Ground
TOWNPARKS
MILVERTON DEMESNE
MILVERTON
HILLSID
osi

INDEX

An Claddagh B2
Arcadia Court C2
Ardgillan View B2
Balbriggan Road B2
Balbriggan Street C2
Beau-Piers Lane C2
Brookville Lane C2
Cabra Hill C3
Callaghan's Lane C2
Chapel Lane C2
Church Street C2
Churchfield Close C3
Churchfield Lawns C3
College Court C2
Convent Lane C2
Downside Heights C3
Downside Park C3
Dublin Road B3
Fox Grove B2
Friar's Lane C2
Greenlawns B3
Harbour Road C2
Harbour Road C1
Harrison's Cove B2
Heeney's Lane C2
Hillside Close C3
Hillside Gardens C3
Holmpatrick C2
Holmpatrick Terrace C3
Kelly's Bay A2
Kelly's Bay Beach A2
Kelly's Bay Cliffs A2
Kelly's Bay Cove A2
Kelly's Bay Drive A2
Kelly's Bay Heights A2
Kelly's Bay Inlet A2
Kelly's Bay Moorings A2
Kelly's Bay Pier A2
Kelly's Bay Promenade A2
Kelly's Bay Rocks A2
Kelly's Bay Shore B2
Kelly's Bay Strand A2
Kelly's Bay Tower A2
Kelly's Bay View A2
Kelly's Bay Weir A2
Little Strand Street C2
Manning's Opening C2
Martine Court C2
Marywell C3
McLoughlin's Lane C2
Miller's Lane C3
Millhill Park C2
Millview C2
Mooring Cove B2
Mourne Close B2
Mourne Court B2
Mourne Drive B2
Mourne Grove B2
Mourne Park B2
Mourne Place B2
Mourne View B2
New Street C2
New Townparks B2
North Strand B2
Northcliffe Heights B2
Quay Street C2
Red Island C2
Rush Road C3
Sandy Banks C2
Seacrest B2
Selskar Avenue B2
Selskar Court B2
Selskar Rise B2
Selskar Road B2
Shalloch Hill Grove B2
Shenick Avenue C3
Shenick Drive C3
Shenick Grove C3
Shenick Park C3
Shenick Road C3
Sherlock Park C3
Sherlock Terrace C3
Skerries Rock Estate B2
South Strand C2
St. Patrick's Close B3
Station Road B3
Strand Street C2
The Avenue, Skerries Rock B2
The Brambles B2
The Court, Skerries Rock B2
The Cresc., Skerries Rock B2
The Cross C2
The Drive, Skerries Rock B2
The Grove, Skerries Rock B2
The Haven C2
The Heights, Skerries Rock B2
The Hoar Rock B2
The Kybe C2
The Lawn, Skerries Rock B2
The Maltings C3
The Park B2
The Park, Skerries Rock B2
The Rise, Skerries Rock B2
The Square B3
The Vale, Skerries Rock B2
The View, Skerries Rock B2
The View, Skerries Rock B2
The Walk, Skerries Rock B2
The Way, Skerries Rock B2
Thomas Hand Street B3
Townparks B2
Townspark B2
Weldon's Lane C3
Windmill Close A2
Windmill Court A2
Windmill Drive A2
Windmill Lane C3

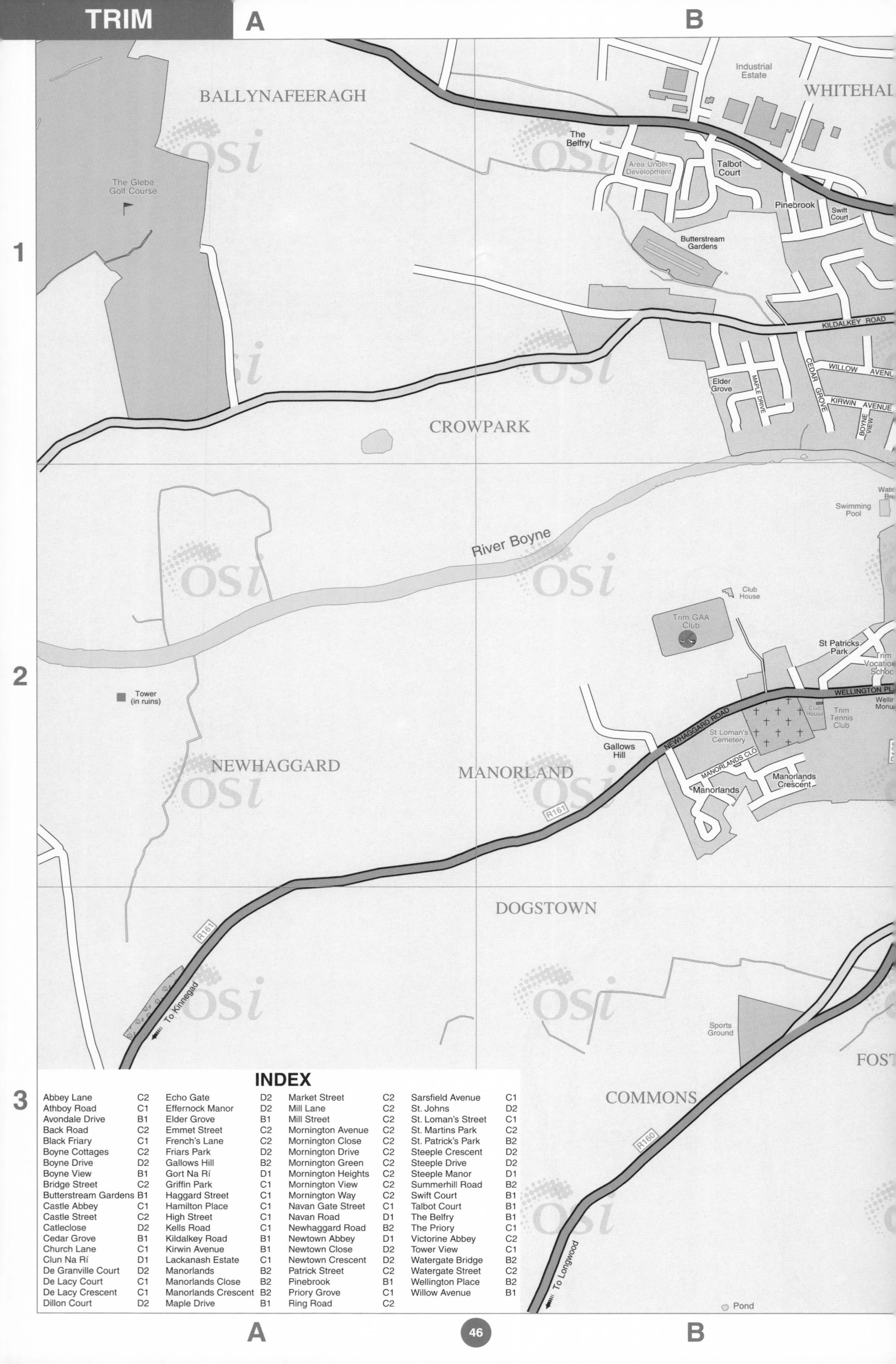

INDEX

Street	Grid	Street	Grid	Street	Grid	Street	Grid
Abbey Lane	C2	Echo Gate	D2	Market Street	C2	Sarsfield Avenue	C1
Athboy Road	C1	Effernock Manor	D2	Mill Lane	C2	St. Johns	D2
Avondale Drive	B1	Elder Grove	B1	Mill Street	C2	St. Loman's Street	C1
Back Road	C2	Emmet Street	C2	Mornington Avenue	C2	St. Martins Park	C2
Black Friary	C1	French's Lane	C2	Mornington Close	C2	St. Patrick's Park	B2
Boyne Cottages	C2	Friars Park	D2	Mornington Drive	C2	Steeple Crescent	D2
Boyne Drive	D2	Gallows Hill	B2	Mornington Green	C2	Steeple Drive	D2
Boyne View	B1	Gort Na Rí	D1	Mornington Heights	C2	Steeple Manor	D1
Bridge Street	C2	Griffin Park	C1	Mornington View	C2	Summerhill Road	B2
Butterstream Gardens	B1	Haggard Street	C1	Mornington Way	C2	Swift Court	B1
Castle Abbey	C1	Hamilton Place	C1	Navan Gate Street	C1	Talbot Court	B1
Castle Street	C2	High Street	C1	Navan Road	D1	The Belfry	B1
Catleclose	D2	Kells Road	C1	Newhaggard Road	B2	The Priory	C1
Cedar Grove	B1	Kildalkey Road	B1	Newtown Abbey	D1	Victorine Abbey	C2
Church Lane	C1	Kirwin Avenue	B1	Newtown Close	D2	Tower View	C1
Clun Na Rí	D1	Lackanash Estate	C1	Newtown Crescent	D2	Watergate Bridge	B2
De Granville Court	D2	Manorlands	B2	Patrick Street	C2	Watergate Street	C2
De Lacy Court	C1	Manorlands Close	B2	Pinebrook	B1	Wellington Place	B2
De Lacy Crescent	C1	Manorlands Crescent	B2	Priory Grove	C1	Willow Avenue	B1
Dillon Court	D2	Maple Drive	B1	Ring Road	C2		

C
D
1
2
3
MMONS
ATHBOY ROAD
TOWER VIEW
KELLS ROAD
Black Friary (In ruins)
Athboy Gate (Site of)
tle Abbey
THE PRIORY
Priory Grove
HAGGARD ST
Griffin Park
De Lacy Crescent
De Lacy Court
Hamilton Place
NAVAN ROAD
GORT NA RI
NEWTOWN
St. Patrick's Cathedral (C of I)
Grave Yard
Church (In ruins)
Black Friary
Lackanash Estate
Clun Na Ri
Steeple Manor
Newtown Abbey
ST LOMAN'S STREET
CHURCH LANE
NAVAN GATE ST
Navan Gate (Site of)
SARSFIELD AVENUE
HIGH STREET
St. Patrick's National School
Nangle Castle (In ruins)
Yellow Tower of St Mary's Abbey (In ruins)
MILL STREET
ABBEY LANE
BRIDGE ST
rer Gate ite of)
Millennium Bridge
BOYNE COTTAGES
Court House
FRENCHES LANE
MARKET STREET
Porch Field
Grave Yard
Church (in ruins)
Newtown Abbey (in ruins)
St. John's Friary (in ruins)
Tower
Sewage Plant
St. Peter's or Newtown Bridge
Town Hall
Medical Centre
Trim Castle (In Ruins)
blin Gate Site of)
St. Patrick's Catholic Church
ercy nvent
CASTLE STREET
Grotto
River Boyne
R154
ECHO GATE
Area Under Construction
Saint Johns
Mercy College
NEWTOWN CLOSE
STEEPLE DRIVE
De Granville Court
Victorine Abbey
Dillon Court
Friars Park
Mary's Girls onal School
Grotto
PATRICK STREET
BACK ROAD
Norman Pratt Memorial Park
NEWTOWN CRESCENT
CRESCENT
BOYNE DRIVE
STEEPLE
Castleclose
Michael's Boys tional School
Burial Ground (Disused)
St Joseph's Hospital
Boyne Community School
R158
RING ROAD
ington Close
INGTON VIEW
MORNINGTON WAY
FRIARSPARK
Effernock Manor
MORNINGTON DRIVE
St Martin's Park
rnington eights
MORNINGTON GREEN
AVE
MORNINGTON
R161
MAUDLIN
R158
TOWN
SHANLOTHE
BROWNSTOWN
To Summerhill
STONEHALL
C
D

INDEX

Abbeylands	C2	Huntsman's Way	C2
Baker's Close	B2	Kelly Park	B2
Balleally Lane	B3	Little Commons	C2
Barrack Lane	B2	Mackerlin Close	B2
Blacksmith's Road	B2	Main Street	B2
Bramble Lane	C2	Miller's Square	B2
Chapel Farm Avenue	B2	Minister's Park	B2
Chapel Farm Close	B2	Minister's Rise	B2
Chapel Farm Court	B3	Minister's Road	B2
Chapel Farm Road	B2	Minister's Road	A2
Chapel Farm Square	B3	Orlynn Park Avenue	B2
Chapel Farm Terrace	B3	Orlynn Park Close	B2
Chapel Lane	B2	Orlynn Park The Drive	B2
Chapel Road	B2	Orlynn Park The Park	B3
Church Road	B2	Post Office Road	B2
Cobbler's Walk	B2	Rogerstown Lane	C3
Coleman's Crescent	B2	Scholar's Walk	B2
Coleman's Way	B2	Skerries Road	B1
Dublin Road	B2	Station Road	B2
Dun Emer Avenue	B2	Stonemason's Close	B2
Dun Emer Close	B2	Stonemason's Road	B2
Dun Emer Court	B2	Sweetman Walk	B2
Dun Emer Drive	A2	Tanner's Way	B2
Dun Emer Gardens	A2	Thatcher's Way	B2
Dun Emer Green	B2	The Green	B2
Dun Emer Lawns	A2	The Square	B2
Dun Emer Park	A2	Tower View	B2
Dun Emer Place	A2	Treen Hill	B2
Dun Emer Road	B2	Tyrell's Row	B2
Dun Emer Way	A2	Village Road	B2
Forge Lane	B2	Weaver's Crescent	B2
Foullard Lane	B2	Whitethorn Walk	C2
Hands Lane	B2	Windward Way	B2
Huntsman's Road	C2		

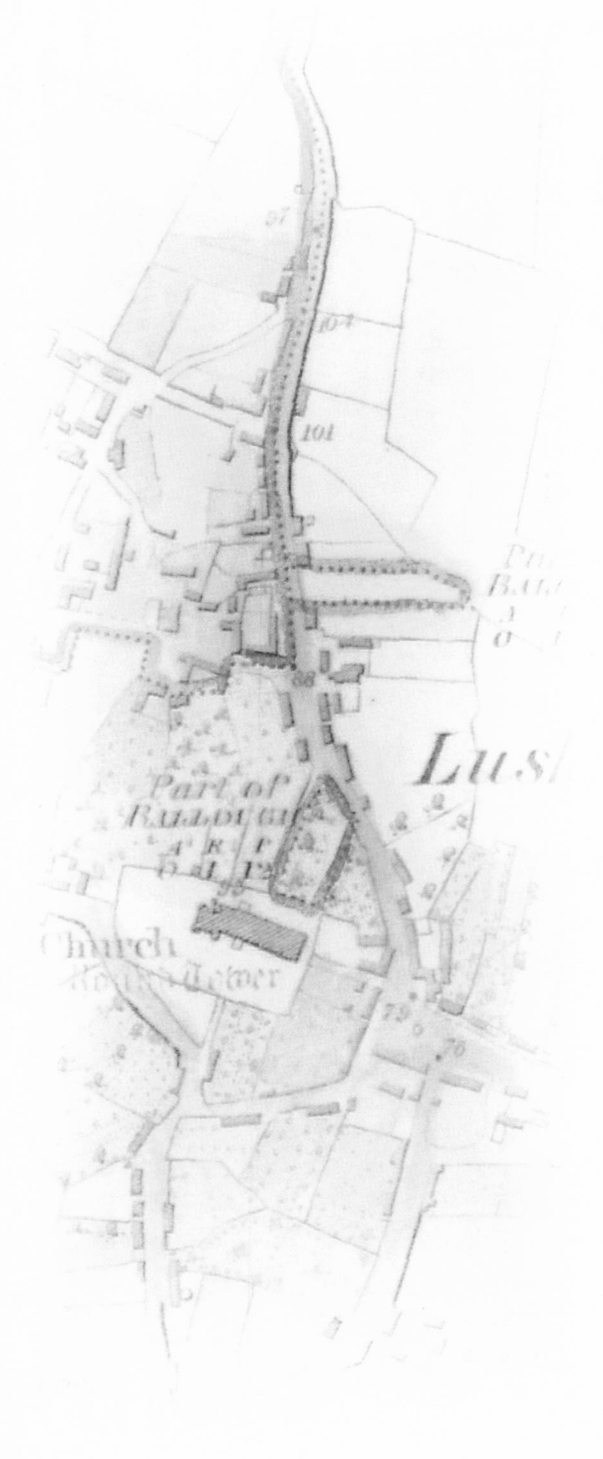

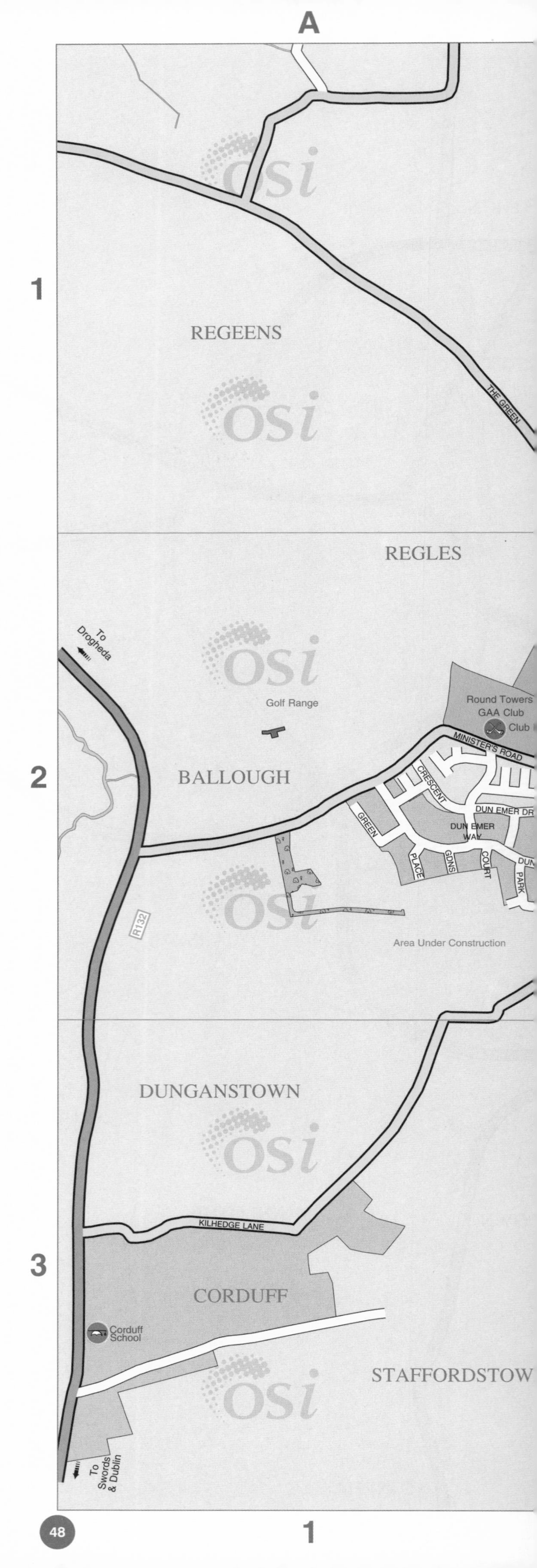

B
C
COLLINSTOWN
RATHMOONEY
To Skerries
R127
GREATCOMMON
CAUSESTOWN
1
TYRRELSTOWN
SKERRIES ROAD
Skerries Road Roundabout
RAHENY
CHAPEL LANE
Church
FOULLARD LANE
Lusk National School
BAKER'S CLOSE
COLEMAN'S CRESCENT & WAY
SCHOLAR'S WALK
FORGE LANE
Abbeylands
THE GREEN
Monastery (Site of)
CHAPEL ROAD
VILLAGE ROAD
MILLER'S SQUARE
WEAVER'S CRES
HUNTSMAN'S ROAD
Little Commons
HUNTSMAN'S WAY
BRAMBLE LANE
Minister's Park
Minister's Rise
TREEN HILL
POST OFFICE ROAD
WHITETHORN WALK
Raheny Roundabout
MINISTER'S ROAD
TOWER VIEW
MAIN STREET
St.Mac Cullins Church
2
MACKERLIN CLOSE
CHURCH ROAD
The Square
DUN EMER GREEN
DUN EMER COURT
DUN EMER ROAD
DUN EMER CLOSE
Lusk United
STATION ROAD
Area Under Construction
BARRACK LANE
AVENUE
CLOSE
Orlynn Park
Community Unit for the Elderly
Area Under Construction
Chapel Farm
DUBLIN ROAD
THE DRIVE
R128
To Rush
THE PARK
Tennis Courts
TERRACE
SQUARE
COURT
RACECOURSE COMMON
ROGERSTOWN LANE
BALLEALLY LANE
3
BRIDETREE
(Site of)
(Site of)
Dublin
R127

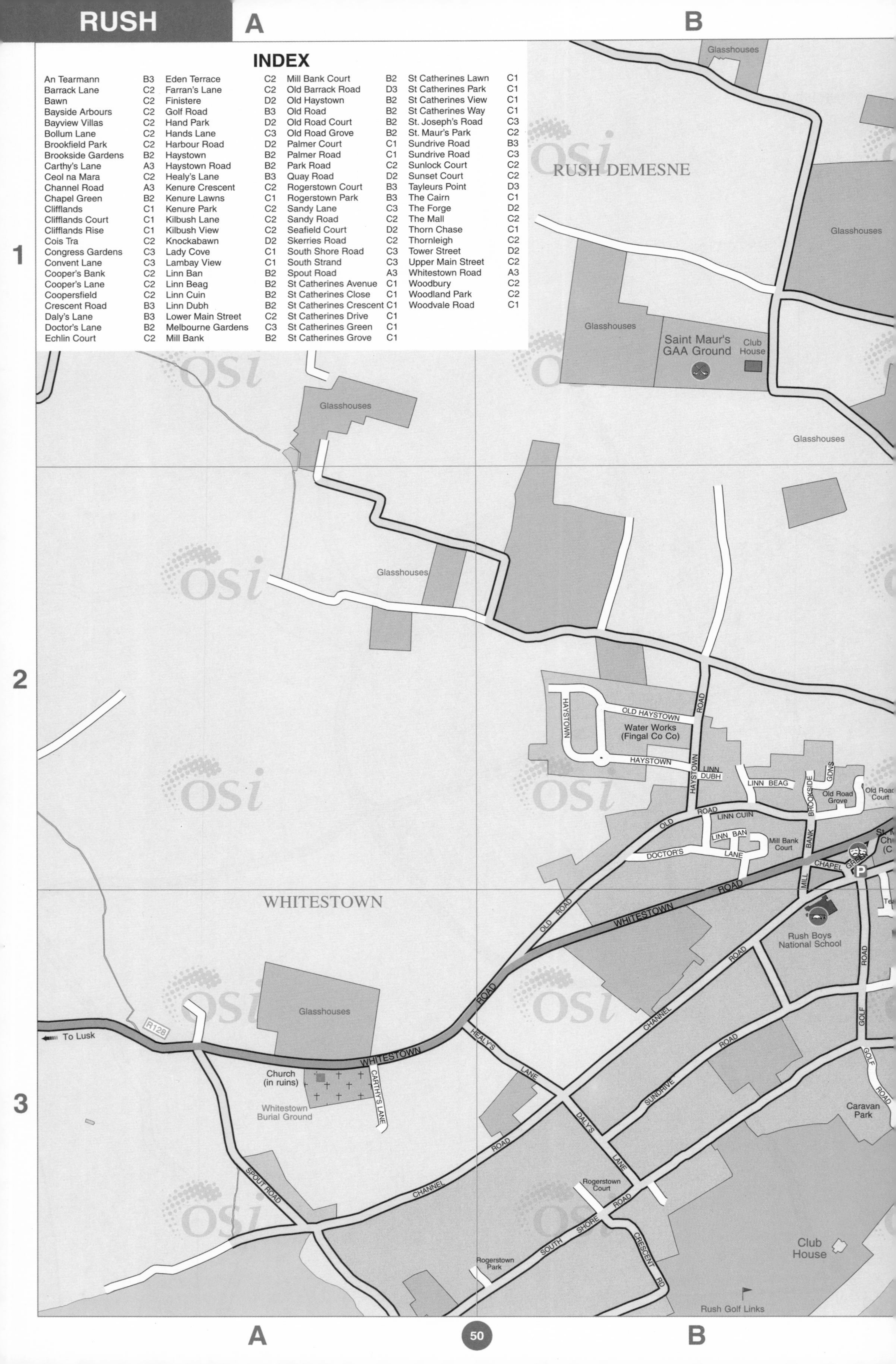

INDEX

An Tearmann B3
Barrack Lane C2
Bawn C2
Bayside Arbours C2
Bayview Villas C2
Bollum Lane C2
Brookfield Park C2
Brookside Gardens B2
Carthy's Lane A3
Ceol na Mara C2
Channel Road A3
Chapel Green B2
Clifflands C1
Clifflands Court C1
Clifflands Rise C1
Cois Tra C2
Congress Gardens C3
Convent Lane C3
Cooper's Bank C2
Cooper's Lane C2
Coopersfield C2
Crescent Road B3
Daly's Lane B3
Doctor's Lane B2
Echlin Court C2
Eden Terrace C2
Farran's Lane C2
Finistere D2
Golf Road B3
Hand Park D2
Hands Lane C3
Harbour Road D2
Haystown B2
Haystown Road B2
Healy's Lane B3
Kenure Crescent C2
Kenure Lawns C1
Kenure Park C2
Kilbush Lane C2
Kilbush View C2
Knockabawn D2
Lady Cove C1
Lambay View C1
Linn Ban B2
Linn Beag B2
Linn Cuin B2
Linn Dubh B2
Lower Main Street C2
Melbourne Gardens C3
Mill Bank B2
Mill Bank Court B2
Old Barrack Road D3
Old Haystown B2
Old Road B2
Old Road Court B2
Old Road Grove B2
Palmer Court C1
Palmer Road C1
Park Road C2
Quay Road D2
Rogerstown Court B3
Rogerstown Park B3
Sandy Lane C3
Sandy Road C2
Seafield Court D2
Skerries Road C2
South Shore Road C3
South Strand C3
Spout Road A3
St Catherines Avenue C1
St Catherines Close C1
St Catherines Crescent C1
St Catherines Drive C1
St Catherines Green C1
St Catherines Grove C1
St Catherines Lawn C1
St Catherines Park C1
St Catherines View C1
St Catherines Way C1
St. Joseph's Road C3
St. Maur's Park C2
Sundrive Road B3
Sundrive Road C3
Sunlock Court C2
Sunset Court C2
Tayleurs Point D3
The Cairn C1
The Forge D2
The Mall C2
Thorn Chase C1
Thornleigh C2
Tower Street D2
Upper Main Street C2
Whitestown Road A3
Woodbury C2
Woodland Park C2
Woodvale Road C1

IRISH SEA
To Skerries
Grave Yard
Church (in ruins)
R128
St. Catherine's Estate
CRESCENT
PARK
GREEN
LAWN
AVENUE
WAY
DRIVE
GROVE
LAMBAY VIEW
VIEW
CLOSE
THE CAIRN
RISE
CLIFFLANDS CT
Saint Catherine's National School
WOODVALE RD
Clifflands
THORN CHASE
Brooks's End
Megalithic Tomb (Site of)
Ravenswell
PALMER
ROAD
PALMER CT
Lady Cove
Caravan Park
Kenure Lawns
KENURE CRES
ST.MAUR'S PARK
Rush Cricket Club
Kenure Church (C of I)
Kenure Park
Kenure Parsonage
Woodbury
PARK
ROAD
Area Under Construction
SKERRIES
ROAD
Caravan Park
KILBUSH
LANE
Kilbush View
Brookfield Park
Sunset Court
FARRAN'S LANE
COOPER'S LANE
SOUTH
Thornleigh
KILBUSH LANE
Seafield Court
Pier
HARBOUR
ROAD
QUAY RD
Coopersfield
Cois Tra
Ceol Na Mara
The Mall
Barrack Lane
The Forge
UPPER
MAIN
STREET
Bayside Arbours
ROAD
Bayview Villas
Echlin Court
BOLLUM LANE
PO
Cooper's Bank
Sunlock Court
BAWN
Dispensary
LOWER
EDEN TCE
MAIN
STREET
Finistere
QUAY
ROAD
TOWER
STREET
Hand Park
Knockabawn
Martello Tower
St Catherines Well
Rush Vocational School
LANE
Tennis Ground
Sisters of Mercy Convent
CONVENT
Tennis Ground
CONGRESS GDNS
MELBOURNE GDNS
OLD
BARRACK
ROAD
Tayleurs Point
SANDY
LANE
ST JOSEPH'S RD
Saint Joseph's Secondary School
SUNDRIVE
ROAD
HANDS
LANE
Caravan Park
Caravan Park
SOUTH STRAND
ROAD
SHORE
ROAD
SOUTH
Caravan Park
1
2
3
osi

INDEX

Ardlea B2
Coldrick's Pass C2
College Close B2
College Green B2
College Grove B2
College Park B2
College Rise B2
Cooksland B2
Drumree Road B2
Eden Court B2
Grange Hall B2
Greenane B2
Hillview Estate B2
Industrial Estate C3
Lagore Court C2
Lagore Green C2
Lagore Road C2
Manor Court B2
Manor Lands B2
Maolduin C2
Navan Road B2
Park Close B2
Redbeg B1
Redbeg Road B1
Seachnaill Place B2
St.Seachnaill's C2
Supple Hall B2
Supple Park B2
The Bog Road B2
The Court B2
The Courtyard C2
The Crescent B2
The Dales B2
The Downs B2
The Elms B2
The Gables B2
The Meadows B2
The Paddock C2
The Rise B3

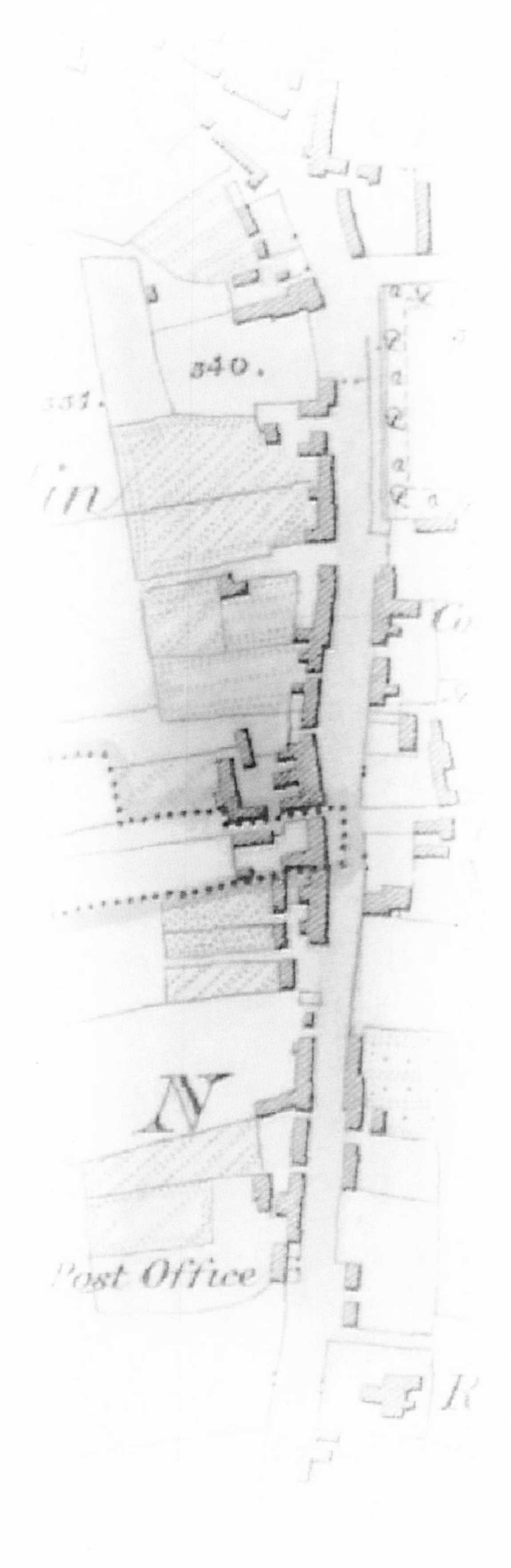

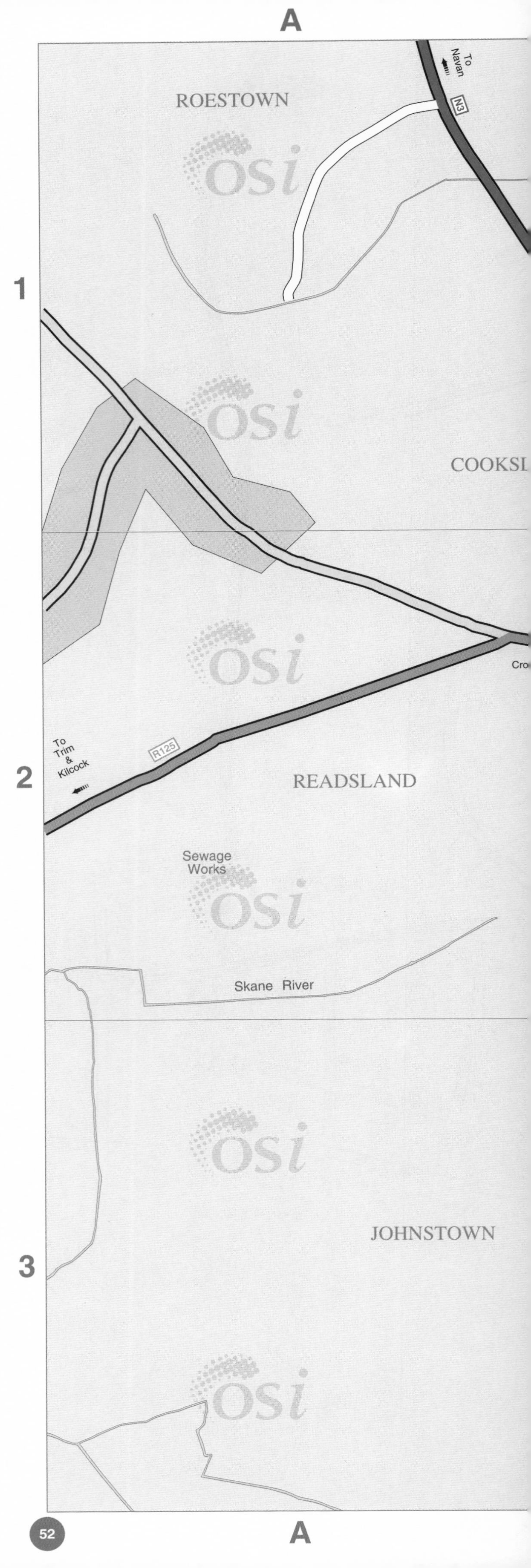

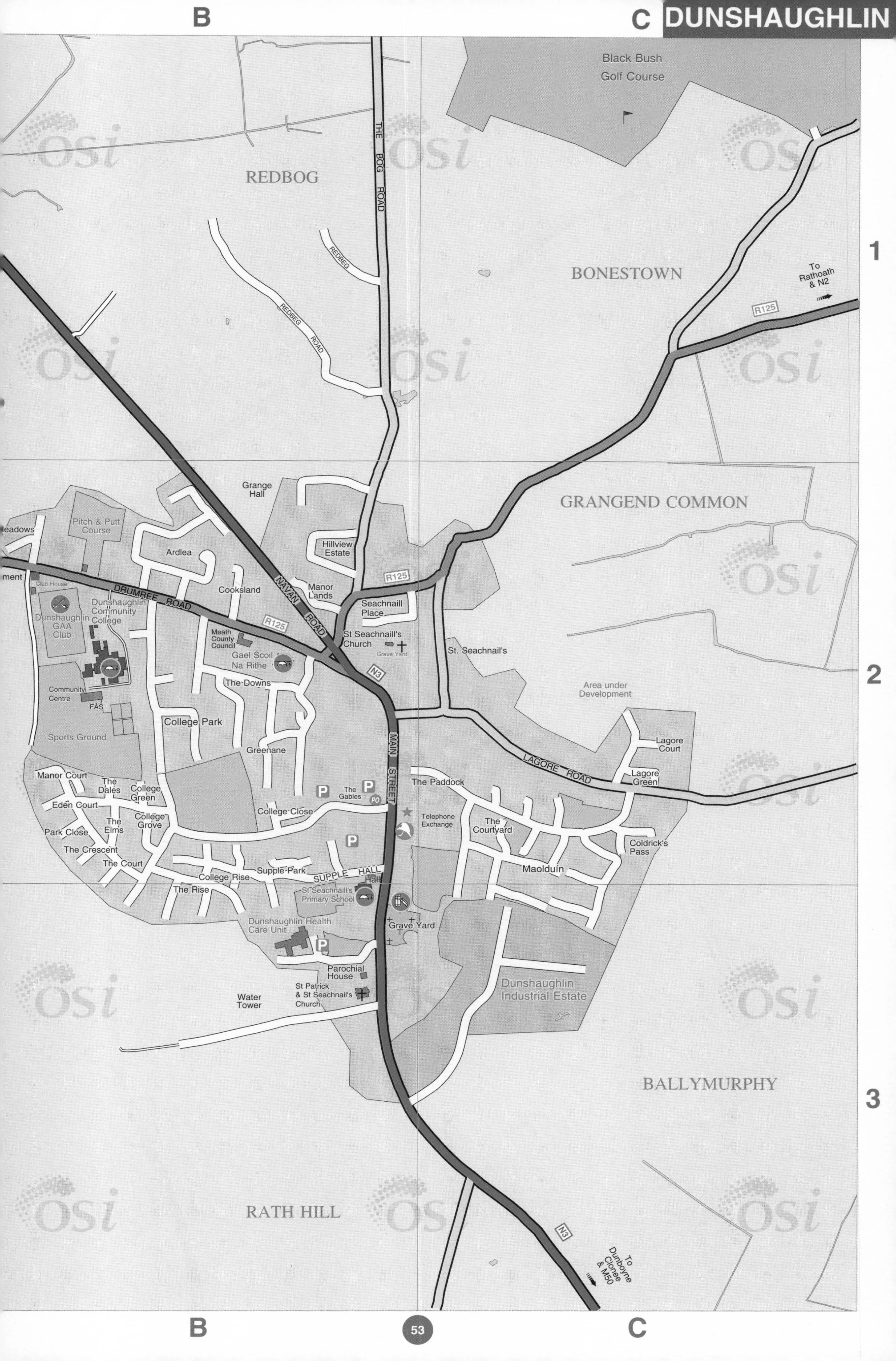
B
C
1
2
3
Black Bush Golf Course
REDBOG
THE BOG ROAD
REDBEG
REDBEG ROAD
BONESTOWN
To Rathoath & N2
R125
GRANGEND COMMON
Grange Hall
Pitch & Putt Course
Hillview Estate
Ardlea
Manor Lands
Cooksland
NAVAN ROAD
DRUMREE ROAD
R125
Club House
Dunshaughlin GAA Club
Dunshaughlin Community College
Meath County Council
Gael Scoil Na Rithe
Seachnaill Place
St Seachnaill's Church
Grave Yard
N3
St. Seachnaill's
Area under Development
The Downs
Community Centre
FAS
Sports Ground
College Park
Greenane
MAIN STREET
Lagore Court
LAGORE ROAD
Lagore Green
Manor Court
The Dales
College Green
Eden Court
Park Close
The Elms
College Grove
The Crescent
The Court
The Gables
PO
College Close
The Paddock
Telephone Exchange
The Courtyard
Coldrick's Pass
Maolduin
Supple Park
SUPPLE HALL
Hall
College Rise
The Rise
St Seachnaill's Primary School
Grave Yard
Dunshaughlin Health Care Unit
Parochial House
St Patrick & St Seachnaill's Church
Water Tower
Dunshaughlin Industrial Estate
BALLYMURPHY
RATH HILL
N3
To Dunboyne Clonee & M50
B
C

INDEX

Street	Grid
Ashbourne Road	D2
Ballybin Road	D2
Beechlawns	C2
Brownstown	B1
Cairn Court	B3
Cairn Manor	B3
Clonkeen	B2
Coill Beag	C2
Corballis Demesne	C1
Dunshaughlin Road	B2
Fairyhouse Lodge	B2
Fairyhouse Road	B3
Fortune Way	B2
Fox Lodge Avenue	C2
Fox Lodge Crescent	C2
Fox Lodge Gardens	C1
Fox Lodge Lane	C2
Fox Lodge Manor	C1
Fox Lodge Road	C2
Fox Lodge Wood	C2
Foxbrook	C1
Glebe Park	C1
Green Hill Bridge	A1
Jamestown Park	C2
Kilbride Road	D3
Leigh Valley	C1
Meadowbank Hill	C2
Milltree Crescent	C2
Mill Tree Park	C2
Mill Tree Park, The Avenue	C2
Mill Tree Park, The Drive	C2
Mill Tree Park, The Grove	C2
Mill Tree Park, The Way	C2
Milltree Rise	C3
Moatlands	B2
Moulden Bridge Estate	A4
Mruigtuaithe	B2
Norman Grove	B1
Park View	B1
Seagrave Hall	B3
Seagrave Park	B2
Skryne Road	B1
Somerville	B2
St. Oliver's Park	B2
Steeplechase Green	B1
Steeplechase Hill	B1
Steeplechase Wood	B1
Streamstown	B1
The Close	C2
The Commons	B3
The Old Mill	C2
The Paddocks	C1
The Village Green	C2
Woodlands	B2
Woodlands Park	B2

C
D
1
2
3
To N2 & Navan
R155
Foxbrook
Leigh Valley
Glebe Park
Corbaillis Demesne
Church (in ruins)
R125
Holy Trinity Church
Motte
Parochial House
Ratoath Manor Nursing Home
Beechlawns
Fox Lodge Woods
Fox Lodge Manor
GARDENS
AVENUE
CRESCENT
LANE
FOX LODGE ROAD
The Close
The Village Green
Sewage Works
Coill Beag
Jamestown Park
St. Paul's National School
THE AVENUE
THE WAY
THE DRIVE
THE GROVE
Mill Tree Park
MILLTREE CRESCENT
MILLTREE RISE
The Old Mill
Fairyhouse Lodge
GLASCAIRN LANE
BALLYBIN
To Ashbourne
BALLYBIN ROAD
Moulden Bridge Estate
ASHBOURNE ROAD
Moulden Bridge
To N2/Ashbourne M50 & Dublin
TANKARDSTOWN
KILBRIDE ROAD
To Kilbride

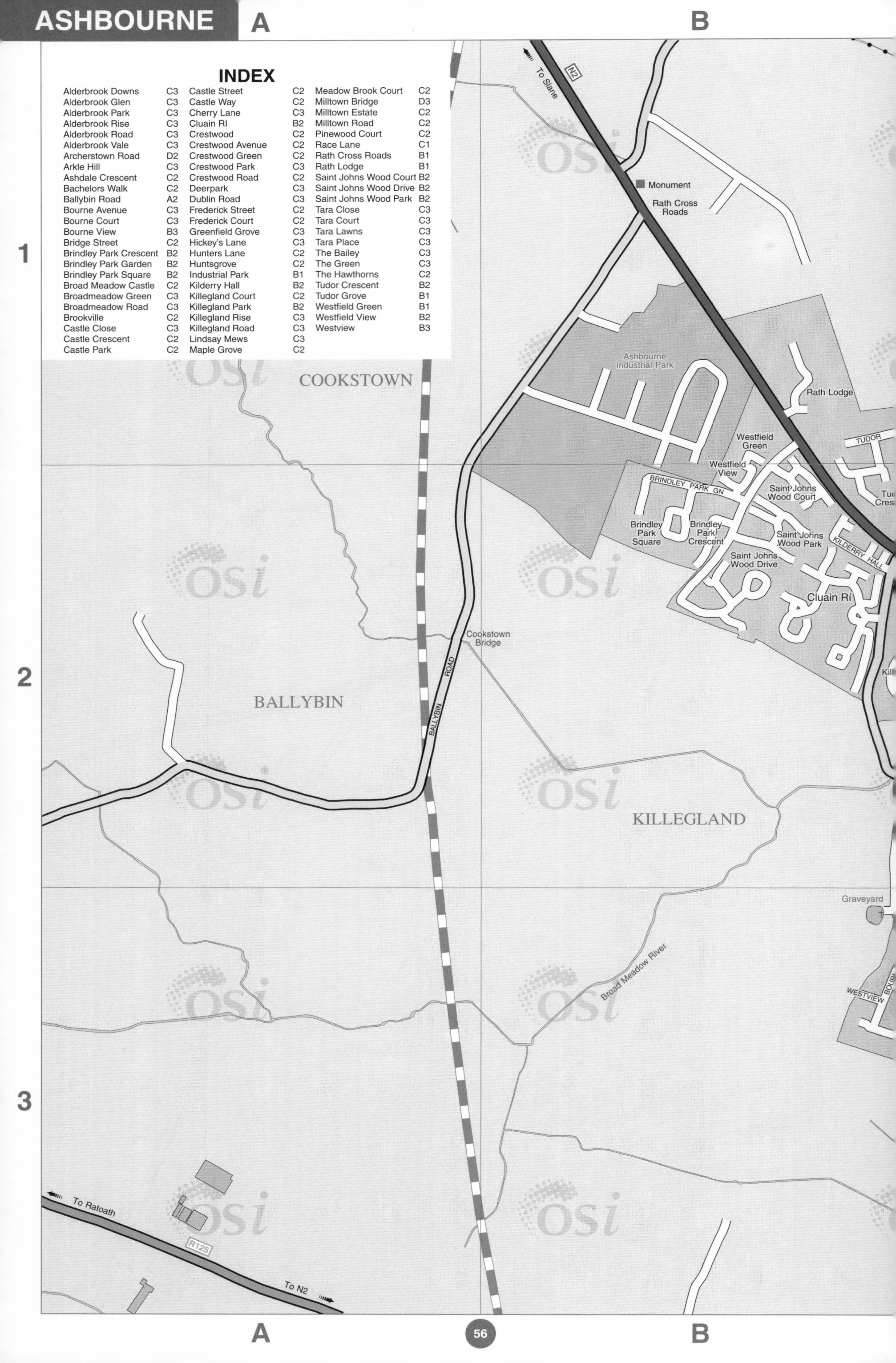

INDEX

Street	Grid	Street	Grid	Street	Grid
Alderbrook Downs	C3	Castle Street	C2	Meadow Brook Court	C2
Alderbrook Glen	C3	Castle Way	C2	Milltown Bridge	D3
Alderbrook Park	C3	Cherry Lane	C3	Milltown Estate	C2
Alderbrook Rise	C3	Cluain RI	B2	Milltown Road	C2
Alderbrook Road	C3	Crestwood	C2	Pinewood Court	C2
Alderbrook Vale	C3	Crestwood Avenue	C2	Race Lane	C1
Archerstown Road	D2	Crestwood Green	C2	Rath Cross Roads	B1
Arkle Hill	C3	Crestwood Park	C3	Rath Lodge	B1
Ashdale Crescent	C2	Crestwood Road	C2	Saint Johns Wood Court	B2
Bachelors Walk	C2	Deerpark	C3	Saint Johns Wood Drive	B2
Ballybin Road	A2	Dublin Road	C3	Saint Johns Wood Park	B2
Bourne Avenue	C3	Frederick Street	C2	Tara Close	C3
Bourne Court	C3	Frederick Court	C2	Tara Court	C3
Bourne View	B3	Greenfield Grove	C3	Tara Lawns	C3
Bridge Street	C2	Hickey's Lane	C3	Tara Place	C3
Brindley Park Crescent	B2	Hunters Lane	C2	The Bailey	C3
Brindley Park Garden	B2	Huntsgrove	C2	The Green	C3
Brindley Park Square	B2	Industrial Park	B1	The Hawthorns	C2
Broad Meadow Castle	C2	Kilderry Hall	B2	Tudor Crescent	B2
Broadmeadow Green	C3	Killegland Court	C2	Tudor Grove	B1
Broadmeadow Road	C3	Killegland Park	B2	Westfield Green	B1
Brookville	C2	Killegland Rise	C3	Westfield View	B2
Castle Close	C3	Killegland Road	C3	Westview	B3
Castle Crescent	C2	Lindsay Mews	C3		
Castle Park	C2	Maple Grove	C2		

C
D
1
2
3
DUNREAGH
Co. DUBLIN
Co. MEATH
MILLTOWN
ARCHERSTOWN
St. Mary's National School
HUNTERS
LANE
TUDOR GROVE
HUNTSGROVE
Brookville
HUNTERS LANE
Ashbourne Town Shopping Centre
FREDERICK STREET
Church of the Immaculate Conception (Cath)
Presbytery
Grave Yard
ASHDALE CRES
MAPLE GRO
MILLTOWN ESTATE
BACHELORS WK
BRIDGE ST
The Hawthorns
Broad Meadow Castle
St. Anthony's
Ashbourne Bridge
Pinewood Court
Sports Ground
CASTLE STREET
MILLTOWN ROAD
ARCHERSTOWN ROAD
Club House
Ashbourne Rugby Club
Meadow Brook Court
FREDERICK COURT
ROAD
CRESTWOOD AVENUE
CASTLE PARK
CASTLE WAY
CASTLE CRES
The Green
DUBLIN ROAD
ALDERBROOK GLEN
Deerpark
CASTLE CLOSE
KILLEGLAND ROAD
Killegland Rise
ALDERBROOK ROAD
Alderbrook Vale
Alderbrook Park
Alderbrook Rise
Alderbrook Downs
AVENUE
BROADMEADOW RD
GREENFIELD GRO
ARKLE HILL
TARA PLACE
Lindsay Mews
Tara Court
Tara Lawns
Tara Close
Broadmeadow Green
BOURNE COURT
Bailey
CHERRY LANE
Ashbourne Community School
Milltown Bridge
Ashbourne Golf Club
Club House
Sports Ground
Pitch and Putt Course
Broad Meadow River
LANE
HICKEY'S
To Finglas
N2

A
B
1
2
3
Rogerstown Estuary
South Shore Rd
Rush Sailing Club
Rush Golf Links
Pier
Porter's Lane
BURROW ROAD
BURROW
Caravan Park
BEACH LANE
LYNDER'S LANE
St. Mochuda's Well
BAHILLION
HEALY'S LANE
Castle (In Ruins)
Catherine's and Longstone Park
To Donabate & N1
R126
The Red Square
The Grey Square
PORTRANE AVENUE
Seaview Park
Tower View Heights
PORTRAINE DEMEN
Portrane House
Church
St Ita's Hospital
Ball Alley
Bowling Green
Recreational Ground
osi

C

IRISH SEA

Martello Tower

P

1

2

3

C

INDEX

Beach Lane	B2	Priest's Chamber	B3
Burrow Road	A1	Seaview Park	B3
Healy's Lane	B2	South Shore Road	A1
Longstone Park	B3	The Grey Square	B3
Lynder's Lane	A2	The Red Square	B3
Porter's Lane	A1	Tower View Heights	B3
Portrane Avenue	B3		

Portraine Ho.

INDEX

Ballisk Court	B2	Eden Grove	B2	The Gallery	B2
Barnewall Avenue	B2	Fairways	C2	The Links	C2
Barnewall Crescent	B2	Hazelwood	B2	The Priory	C2
Beaverbrook	C1	Lambourne Park	C2	The Spires	C2
Beaverstown Orchard	B2	Main Street	B2	The Strand	C3
Beverton Close	B2	Newbridge Avenue	B3	Turvey Avenue	A2
Beverton Court	B2	Orchard Close	C2	Turvey Close	B2
Beverton Crescent	B2	Portrane Road	C2	Turvey Crescent	B2
Beverton Drive	B2	Portrane Road Upper	C2	Turvey Drive	B2
Beverton Green	B2	Priory Wood	C2	Turvey Garden	B2
Beverton Grove	B2	Prospect Hill	B3	Turvey Grove	B2
Beverton Lawn	B2	Somerton	C2	Turvey Park	B2
Beverton Park	B2	St. Mary's Terrace	C3	Turvey Woods	B2
Beverton Way	B2	St. Patrick's Park	C3	Willowbrook	C2
Chapel View	B3	St. Patrick's Terrace	C3		
Cois Inbhir	C2	Station Court	B3		

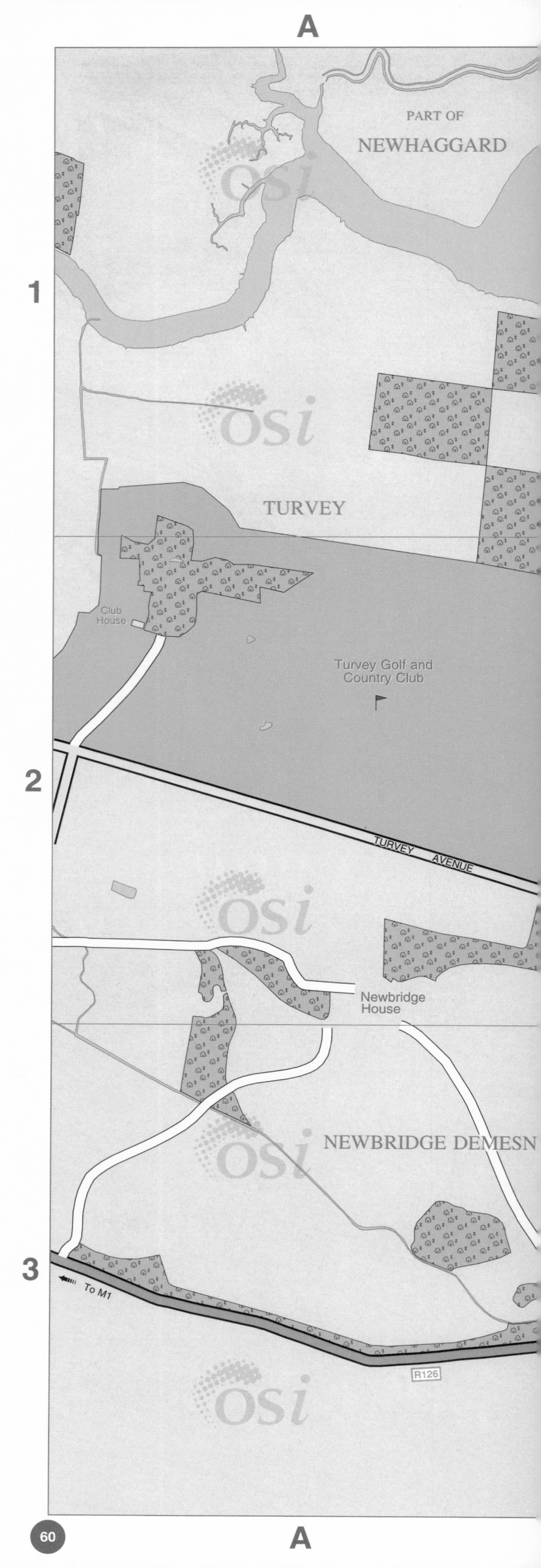

B
C
Rogerstown Estuary
Rogerstown Viaduct
Raheen Point
Dublin/Belfast Railway
Foran's Wells
1
Windmill (in Ruins)
Club House
BEAVERSTOWN
RAHILLION
Beaverstown Golf Course
BEAVERBROOK
Cois Inbhir
Beaverstown Orchard
Orchard Close
Eden Grove
Lambourne Park
St. Patrick's Girls National School
R126
To Portraine
ROAD
PORTRAINE
Somerton
Barnewall
AVE
CRES
The Priory
BALLISK COMMON
WILLOWBROOK
GREEN
LAWN
CRES
WAY
HAZELWOOD
Donabate Community Centre
UPPER
PRIORY
WOOD
2
Beverton Court
DRIVE
GROVE
BEVERTON
Turvey
ROAD
PORTRAINE
The Links
BALLALEASE NORTH
CLOSE
PARK
WOODS
GARDEN
DRIVE
CLO
PARK
CRES
MAIN STREET
BALLISK COURT
The Gallery
GROVE
Donabate
FAIRWAYS
St. Patrick's Church (Cath)
Donabate Rail Station
THE SPIRES
BALLISK
Church (Episcopal) on Site of Church
St Patricks Terrace
St Patricks Park
BALLYMASTONE
NEWBRIDGE AVE
St Mary's Terrace
Chapel View
Station Court
Donabate Golf Club
THE STRAND
Prospect Hill
BALLALEASE SOUTH
DONABATE
3
CORBALLIS
Dublin/Belfast Railway
Donabate Golf Club
B
C

INDEX

Abbeylea Avenue C3
Abbeylea Close C3
Abbeylea Drive C3
Abbeylea Green C3
Abbeyvale Avenue B3
Abbeyvale Close B3
Abbeyvale Court B3
Abbeyvale Crescent B3
Abbeyvale Drive B3
Abbeyvale Green B4
Abbeyvale Grove B3
Abbeyvale Lawn B3
Abbeyvale Place B3
Abbeyvale Rise B3
Abbeyvale View B4
Abbeyvale Way B4
Abington F5
Airside Business Park D5
Applewood Ave East C2
Applewood Ave West C2
Applewood Avenue C2
Applewood Close C2
Applewood Court C2
Applewood Crescent C2
Applewood Drive C2
Applewood Grove C2
Applewood Main St C2
Applewood Mews C2
Applewood Place C2
Applewood Square C2
Ardcian Park C3
Ashdale Close E5
Ashdale Road E5
Ashe Court E5
Ashley Ave D4
Ashley Drive D4
Ashley Grove D4
Aspen Drive E5
Aspen Park E5
Aspen Road E5
Asthown Avenue C2
Asthown Close C2
Asthown Court C2
Asthown Drive C2
Asthown Green C2
Asthown Grove C2
Asthown Lawns C2
Asthown Rise C2
Balheary Industrial Park D2
Balheary Bridge D2
Balheary Road D3
Ballintrane Wood C4
Ballymadrough Road F3
Barry's Park D4
Bell's Lane C4
Berwick Avenue B4
Berwick Court B3
Berwick Crescent B3
Berwick Drive B3
Berwick Grove B3
Berwick Lawn B3
Berwick Place B3
Berwick Rise B4
Berwick View B3
Berwick Walk B4
Berwick Way B3
Birchdale Close E5
Birchdale Drive E5
Birchdale Park F5
Birchdale Road E5
Blakeney House E4
Bolton Green A4
Boroimhe Alder C5
Boroimhe Ash C5
Boroimhe Aspen B5
Boroimhe Beech C5
Boroimhe Birches C5
Boroimhe Blackthorn C5
Boroimhe Cedars C5
Boroimhe Cherry C5
Boroimhe Elms C5
Boroimhe Hawthorns C5
Boroimhe Hazel C5
Boroimhe Laurels C5
Boroimhe Maples C5
Boroimhe Oaks C5
Boroimhe Pines C5
Boroimhe Poplars C5
Boroimhe Rowan B5
Boroimhe Willows C5
Brackenstown Avenue C4
Brackenstown Road A4
Braeburn Terrace C2
Bramley Terrace C2
Bride's Glen Avenue C2
Bride's Glen Park C3
Bridge Street D4
Broadmeadow C3
Broadmeadow Road C3
Brookdale Avenue B4
Brookdale Close B4
Brookdale Court B4
Brookdale Drive B4
Brookdale Green B4
Brookdale Grove B4
Brookdale Lawns B4
Brookdale Park B4
Brookdale Road B4
Brookdale Walk B4
Brookdale Way B4
Bunbury Gate Avenue B2
Bunbury Gate Crescent B2
Carlton Court D4
Carnegie Court Avenue D3
Carwell Court E4
Castle Avenue D4
Castle Downs Croft F4
Castle Downs Grove F4
Castle Downs Road F4
Castle Drive D4
Castle Grove D4
Castle Lawns F4
Castle Park D4
Castlefarm C3
Castlegrange Avenue D3
Castlegrange Close D3
Castlegrange Green D3
Castlegrange Heights D3
Castlegrange Hill D3
Castlegrange Road D3
Castlegrange Way D3
Castleheath F5
Castleview Lawns B2
Castleview Avenue C2
Castleview Close C2
Castleview Court B2
Castleview Crescent C2
Castleview Drive C2
Castleview Green B2
Castleview Grove C2
Castleview Heath B2
Castleview Heights C2
Castleview Meadows C2
Castleview Park C2
Castleview Place C2
Castleview Row C2
Castleview Walk C2
Castleview Way B2
Ceder Park B5
Ceder Square B5
Ceder View B5
Chamley Park F5
Chapel Lane D4
Cherry Avenue C5
Cherry Forest B5
Cherry Garth C4
Cherry Park C5
Church Road D4
Cianlea B3
Clifford's Lane E4
Cooldríona Court D4
Cook's Road A6
Daleview Road C3
Damer House E4
Drynam Ave E6
Drynam Avenue E5
Drynam Close E6
Drynam Copse E6
Drynam Court D4
Drynam Crescent E5
Drynam Drive E5
Drynam Glen E5
Drynam Green E5
Drynam Grove E5
Drynam Hall E5
Drynam Mews E6
Drynam Place E6
Drynam Rise E6
Drynam Road D4
Drynam Square E5
Drynam View E5
Drynam Walk E5
Drynam Way E5
Dublin Road C4
Dublin Street D4
Elmwood Court C3
Elmwood Drive C3
Elmwood Park C3
Elmwood Rd C3
Estuary Court D3
Estuary Road F3
Estuary Walk F4
Eyre Court E5
Feltrim Industrial Park E5
Feltrim Road E5
Forest Avenue B5
Forest Boulevard B5
Forest Court B5
Forest Crescent B5
Forest Dale B5
Forest Drive B5
Forest Fields B5
Forest Fields Road C5
Forest Green B5
Forest Grove B4
Forest Hills C5
Forest Park B4
Forest View B5
Forest Walk B5
Forest Way C5
Forrest Road C5
Forster Way E5
Foxwood D4
Gainsborough Avenuve F5
Gainsborough Close F5
Gainsborough Court F5
Gainsborough Crescent F5
Gainsborough Downs F5
Gainsborough Green F5
Gainsborough Lawn F5
Gainsborough Park F5
Gallows Hill C4
Gartan Court E3
Gartan Drive E3
Glasmore Park C3
Glen Ellan Ave C3
Glen Ellan Close C3
Glen Ellan Court C3
Glen Ellan Crescent C3
Glen Ellan Drive C3
Glen Ellan Gardens C3
Glen Ellan Green C3
Glen Ellan Grove C3
Glen Ellan Park C3
Glen Ellan Pines C3
Glen Ellan Walk C3
Grove Court A4
Hawthorn Park C4
Hearse Road E1
Highfield Close C4
Highfield Crescent C4
Highfield Downs C4
Highfield Green C4
Highfield Lawn C4
Hilltown Close C4
Hilltown Court C4
Hilltown Crescent A4
Hilltown Green C4
Hilltown Grove C4
Hilltown Lawn C4
Hilltown Park C4
Hilltown Road C4
Hilltown Way C4
Hollywell Avenue E5
Hollywell Court D5
Hollywell Crescent D5
Hollywell Drive D5
Hollywell Gardens D5
Holywell Grove E5
Hollywell Heath D5
Hollywell Park E5
Hollywell Place E5
Hollywell Road D5
Hollywell Square E5
Hollywell View E5
Hollywell Walk E5
Hollywell Wood D5
Hutchinson's Strand E3
Jugback Close C3
Jugback Court C3
Jugback Crescent C3
Jugback Green C2
Jugback Lane C3
Kettles Drive E6
Kettles Lane E6
Kettles Place E6
Killeck A4
Killeen Avenue F5
Killeen Court F5
Killeen Crescent F5
Killeen Park F5
Kings Hall E4
Kinsealy Court F5
Kinsealy Downs E5
Knocksedan Bridge A4
Knocksedan Drive A4
Knocksedan Wood A4
Lakeshore Drive D5
Laurelton C3
Lincoln Hall C2
Lioscian B3
Lissadel Crescent F4
Lissadel Grove F4
Lissadel Park F4
Lissadel Wood F4
Lissen Hall E3
Lissen Hall Ave D3
Lissen Hall Bridge D2
Lissen Hall Bridges D2
Lissen Hall Court D3
Lissen Hall Drive E3
Lissen Hall Park E3
Longlands D4
Main Street D4
Malahide Road E4
Mantua Park D3
Melrose Park The Avenue E5
Melrose Park The Close E5
Melrose Park The Cresc. E5
Melrose Park The Drive E5
Melrose Park The Green E5
Melrose Park The Grove E5
Melrose Park The Heights E5
Melrose Park The Lawn E5
Melrose Park The Park E5
Melrose Park The Rise E5
Melrose Park The Villa E5
Melrose Park The Walk E5
Milesian Ave E4
Milesian Court E4
Milesian Grove E4
Milesian Lawn E4
Milton Hall C4
Milton Terrace D4
Moat Lane A4
Molesworth Close A4
Mooretown Avenue C3
Mooretown Grove C3
Mooretown Park C3
Mooretown Road C3
Mount Drinan Avenue E5
Mount Drinan Crescent E5
Mount Drinan Grove E5
Mount Drinan Lawn E5
Mount Drinan Park E5
Mountgorry Way E4
Mount Drinan Walk E5
Naul Road A6
Nethercross Court D1
Nevinstown Lane D5
Newcourt D3
Newcourt Mews D3
Newtown Cottages C2
North Street D3
North Street D4
Oaklands Avenue D4
Oaklands Park D4
Oakwood Avenue C4
Old Brazil Way A4
Old Fort Road A4
Old Yellow Walls Road F4
Ormond Avenue B3
Ormond Close B3
Ormond Crescent B3
Ormond Drive B3
Ormond Grove B3
Ormond Lawn B3
Ormond View B3
Ormond Way B3
Oulart C5
Park Avenue B4
Park View B4
Pine Grove Park C3
Pine Grove Road C3
Pipe Hill C4
Plunket Hall E4
Rathbeal Cottages B2
Rathbeale Court C3
Rathbeale Crescent C3
Rathbeale Rise C4
Rathbeale Road B3
Rathingle Road B5
Ridgewood Avenue B5
Ridgewood Close B5
Ridgewood Court B5
Ridgewood Green B5
Ridgewood Grove B5
Ridgewood Park B5
Ridgewood Place B5
Ridgewood Square B5
River Mall D4
River Valley Avenue C4
River Valley Close B4
River Valley Court B4
River Valley Drive C4
River Valley Grove C5
River Valley Heights C4
River Valley Lawn C4
River Valley Park C4
River Valley Rise C5
River Valley Road C4
River Valley View B4
River Valley Way C4
Rockingham Terrace D4
Russell House E4
Russell's Mews E5
Russell's Place E5
Russell's Terrace E6
Saint Cronan's Avenue C3
Saint Cronan's Close B4
Saint Cronan's Cottages C4
Sandford Wood C2
Seabury Avenue F4
Seabury Close F4
Seabury Court F4
Seabury Crescent F4
Seabury Dale F4
Seabury Downs F4
Seabury Gardens F4
Seabury Glen F4
Seabury Green F4
Seabury Grove F4
Seabury Heights F4
Seabury Lane F4
Seabury Lawns F4
Seabury Meadows F4
Seabury Orchard F4
Seabury Parade F4
Seabury Park F4
Seabury Place F4
Seabury Road F4
Seabury Vale F4
Seabury View F4
Seabury Walk F4
Seabury Wood F4
Seamount View E4
Seatown Business Park E3
Seatown Lane E3
Seatown Park The Avenue D3
Seatown Park The Court D3
Seatown Park The Cresc. D3
Seatown Park The Drive D3
Seatown Park The Green D3
Seatown Park The Grove D3
Seatown Road D3
Seatown Terrace D4
Seatown Villas D3
Seatown Walk D4
Seatown West D3
South Bank C3
St Andrews Park C3
St Columba's Heights C4
St Columba's Rise C4
St Columcille Court D4
St Columcille's Crescent D4
St Columcille's Drive D4
St Columcille's Park D4
St Cronan's Close B4
St Cronan's Court B3
St Cronan's Grove C3
St Cronan's Lawn B3
St Cronan's View B4
St Cronan's Way C4
St Werburgh's Apts E4
Streamstown Lane F6
Swords Buisness Park D4
Swords Business Campus D2
Swords Manor Avenue B4
Swords Manor Court B3
Swords Manor Crescent B3
Swords Manor Drive B3
Swords Manor Grove B4
Swords Manor View B3
Swords Manor Way B3
Talbot Avenue F5
Talbot Hall C2
Talbot Park F5
Talbot Road F5
The Courtyard A4
The Crescent D4
The Green C3
The Nurseries C5
The Oaks B5
The Paddocks D4
The Warren F5
Thornleigh Avenue C2
Thornleigh Close C2
Thornleigh Court C2
Thornleigh Green C2
Thornleigh Lane C2
Thornleigh Park C2
Thornleigh Place C2
Thornleigh Road C2
Thornleigh Row C2
Thornleigh Square C2
Thornleigh Terrace C2
Tudor Court F4
Usher Lane A4
Valley View B3
Walton Hall C2
Waterside Avenue E4
Waterside Close E5
Waterside Court E4
Waterside Crescent E4
Waterside Drive E4
Waterside Green E5
Waterside Kings Hall E4
Waterside Lawn E4
Waterside Park E5
Waterside Place E5
Waterside Rise E4
Waterside Road E4
Waterside Walk E4
Waterside Way E4
Watery Lane D3
Weathercross Court D3
Well Road D4
Wikeford Hall C2
Windmill Avenue C4
Windmill Crescent A4
Windmill Lands C4
Windmill Rise C4

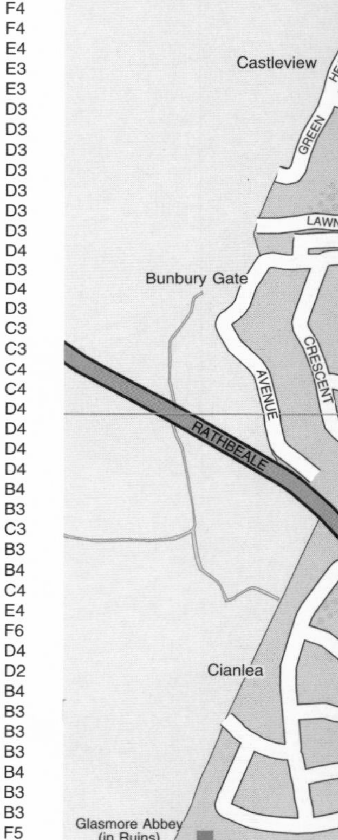

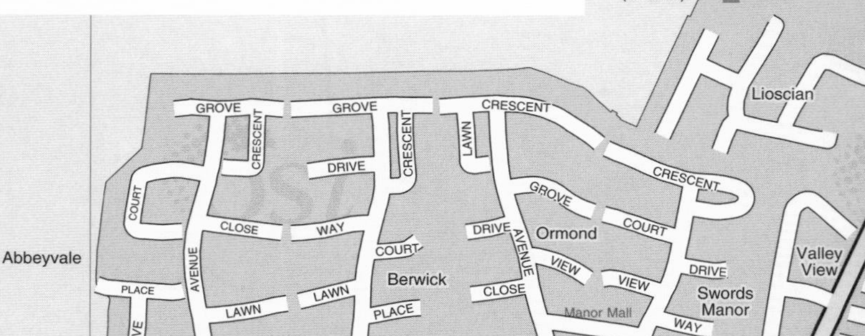

C
D
1
2
3
JAMESTOWN
BALHEARY
Balheary Catholic Church
Balheary Golf Course
LISSENHALL LITTLE
PART of NEWTOWN
NEWTOWN
Weir
NEWTOWN COTTAGES
Club House
Swords Celtic Football Club
Newtown Bridge
St. Mary's Novitiate
BALHEARY DEMESNE
Lissen Hall Bridge
Swords Business Campus
Balheary Bridge
Lissenhall Bridges
Thornleigh
Talbot Hall
Walton Hall
Wikeford Hall
Lincoln Hall
Thornleigh Square
Applewood Square
Applewood Mews
Applewood Court
Jugback Green
JUGBACK LANE
Sandford Wood
Bride's Glen Avenue
Bride's Glen Park
Laurelton
Glen Ellan Green
St Andrews Park
South Bank
Jugback
St. Colmcille G.A.C.
Castlegrange
St. Finian's Community College
BALHEARY ROAD
BALHEARY INDUSTRIAL PARK
Sports Ground
Fingallians GAA Club
Club House
Swords Wastewater Treatment Plant
FB
Broadmeadow
BROADMEADOWS ROAD
Fingal Co. Council Water & Drainage Depot
Fingal Co. Council Housing Maintenance Division
Fingal Co. Council Environmental Division
NTDI Training Centre
WATERY LANE
Castlefarm
Swords Shopping Centre
Caravan Park
RATHBEALE ROAD
RATHBEALE CRESCENT
Glasmore Park
Elmwood Court
Tennis Ground
Tower (in ruins)
NORTH STREET
SEATOWN WEST
Weathercross Court
Seatown Villas
Fingal Community College
SEATOWN ROAD
Seatown Park
NEWCOURT
ESTUARY COURT
SEATOWN ROAD
Swords Business Park
MANTUA PARK
CARNEGIE COURT AVENUE
PINE GROVE PARK
DALEVIEW ROAD
ELMWOOD PARK
ABBEYLEA CLOSE
MOORETOWN ROAD

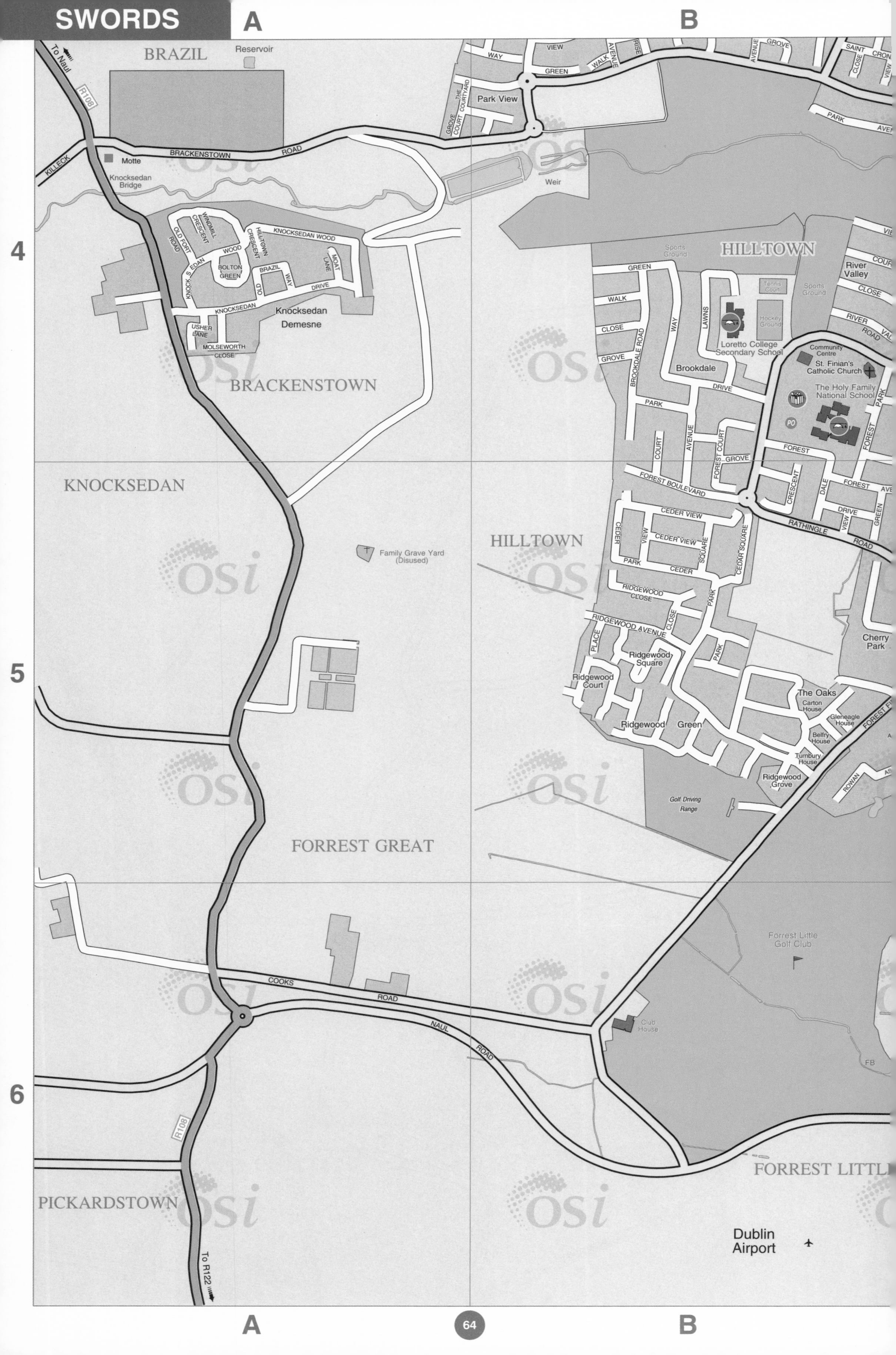
A
B
4
5
6
To Naul
R108
BRAZIL
Reservoir
Motte
KILLECK
BRACKENSTOWN ROAD
Knocksedan Bridge
Weir
Park View
VIEW
WAY
GREEN
WALK
AVENUE
RISE
GROVE
COURT
THE COURTYARD
SAINT
CLOSE
CRON
PARK
OLD FORT ROAD
CRESCENT
WINDMILL
HILLTOWN CRESCENT
KNOCKSEDAN WOOD
WOOD
KNOCK S EDAN
BOLTON GREEN
BRAZIL
MOAT LANE
WAY
DRIVE
KNOCKSEDAN
Knocksedan Demesne
USHER LANE
MOLSEWORTH CLOSE
BRACKENSTOWN
HILLTOWN
Sports Ground
Tennis Court
Hockey Ground
River Valley
CLOSE
RIVER
ROAD
GREEN
WALK
CLOSE
GROVE
BROOKDALE ROAD
WAY
LAWNS
Loretto College Secondary School
Brookdale
Community Centre
St. Finian's Catholic Church
The Holy Family National School
PO
DRIVE
PARK
COURT
AVENUE
FOREST COURT
GROVE
FOREST
FOREST BOULEVARD
CRESCENT
DALE
FOREST
DRIVE
VIEW
GREEN
RATHINGLE ROAD
KNOCKSEDAN
CEDER VIEW
CEDER
VIEW
CEDER VIEW
SQUARE
CEDAR SQUARE
PARK
CEDER
Family Grave Yard (Disused)
HILLTOWN
RIDGEWOOD CLOSE
RIDGEWOOD AVENUE
CLOSE
PARK
PLACE
Ridgewood Square
Ridgewood Court
PARK
Cherry Park
The Oaks
Carton House
Gleneagle House
Belfry House
Turnbury House
FOREST
Ridgewood Green
Ridgewood Grove
ROWAN
Golf Driving Range
FORREST GREAT
Forrest Little Golf Club
COOKS ROAD
NAUL ROAD
Club House
FB
R108
FORREST LITTL
PICKARDSTOWN
Dublin Airport
To R122

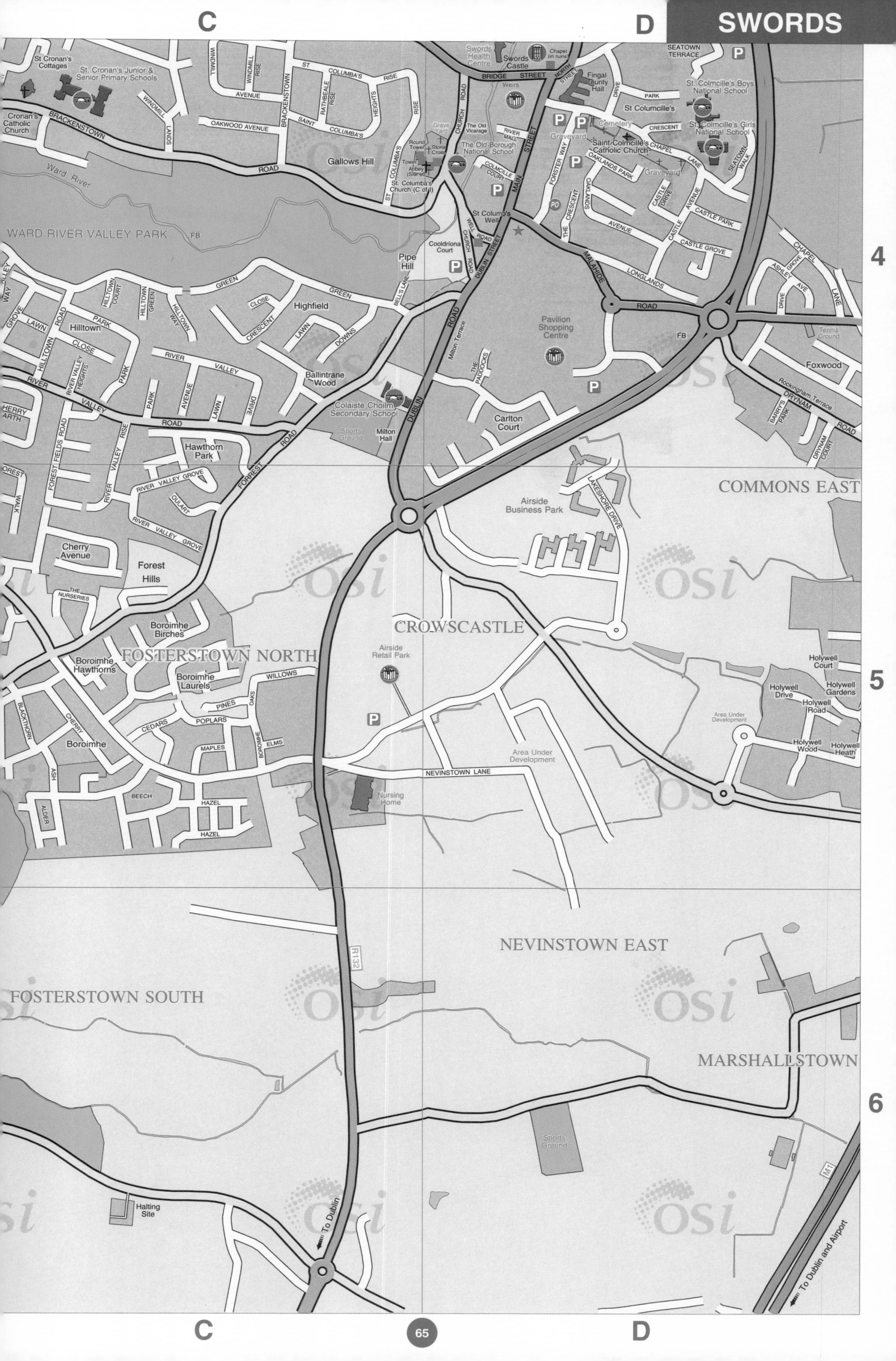
C
D
4
5
6
SWORDS
St Cronan's Cottages
St. Cronan's Junior & Senior Primary Schools
St. Cronan's Catholic Church
BRACKENSTOWN ROAD
Ward River
WARD RIVER VALLEY PARK
Gallows Hill
Swords Health Centre
Swords Castle
Chapel (in ruins)
BRIDGE STREET
NORTH STREET
MAIN STREET
Fingal County Hall
Weirs
St. Columba's Church (C of I)
The Old Borough National School
St Columba's Well
Cooldriona Court
Pipe Hill
Highfield
Hilltown
Ballintrane Wood
Colaiste Choilm Secondary School
Milton Hall
Pavilion Shopping Centre
Carlton Court
MALAHIDE ROAD
St Columcille's
St. Colmcille's Boys National School
St. Colmcille's Girls National School
Saint Colmcille's Catholic Church
SEATOWN TERRACE
Foxwood
Rockingham Terrace
DRYNAM ROAD
COMMONS EAST
Airside Business Park
LAKESHORE DRIVE
Hawthorn Park
Cherry Avenue
Forest Hills
FORREST ROAD
DUBLIN ROAD
CROWSCASTLE
Airside Retail Park
FOSTERSTOWN NORTH
Boroimhe Birches
Boroimhe Hawthorns
Boroimhe Laurels
Boroimhe
NEVINSTOWN LANE
Nursing Home
Area Under Development
Holywell Court
Holywell Drive
Holywell Gardens
Holywell Road
Holywell Wood
Holywell Heath
NEVINSTOWN EAST
FOSTERSTOWN SOUTH
MARSHALLSTOWN
R132
Sports Ground
Halting Site
To Dublin
M1
To Dublin and Airport

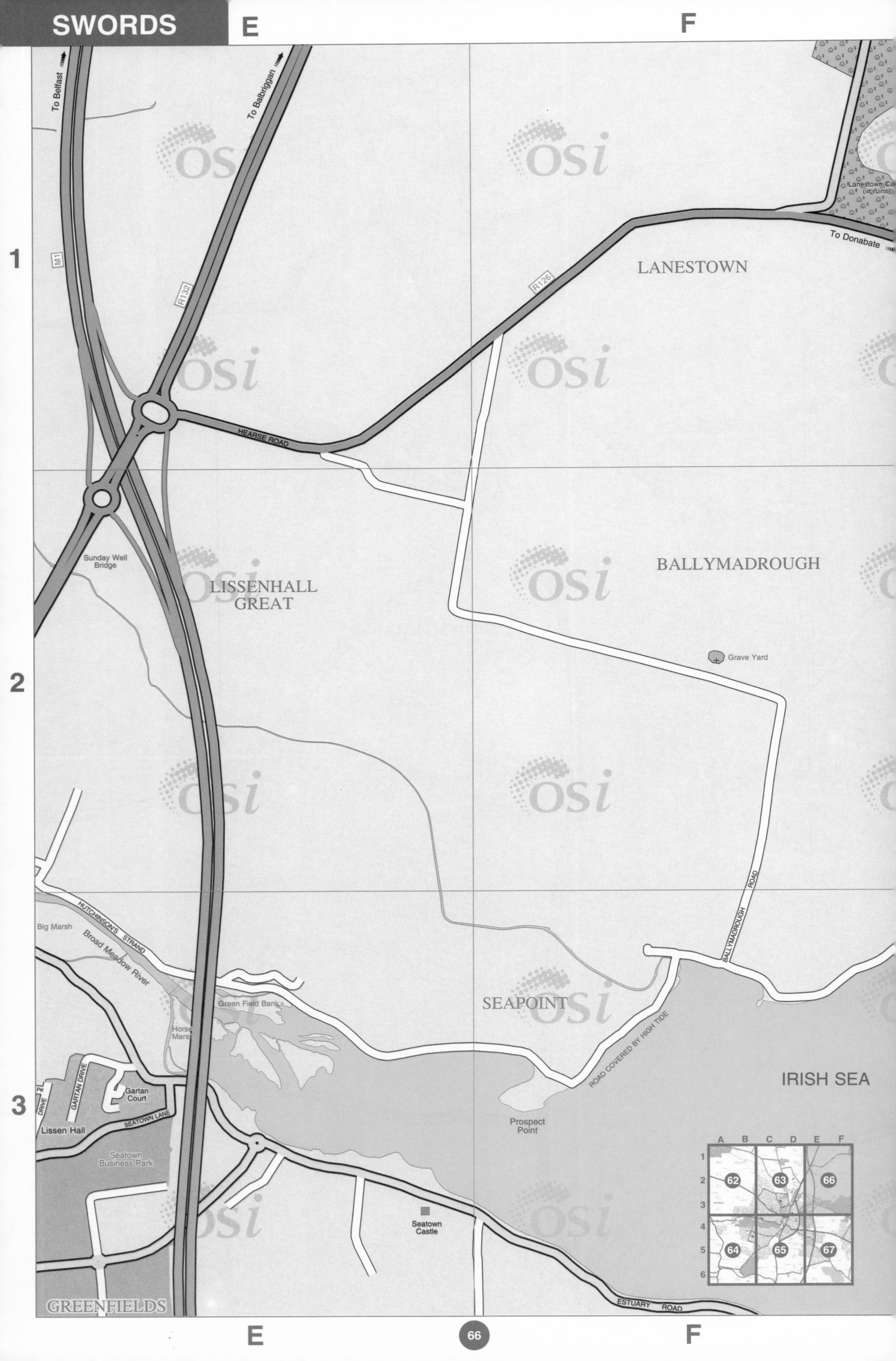
E
F
To Belfast
To Balbriggan
M1
R132
R126
HEARSE ROAD
To Donabate
Lanestown Ca
(in ruins)
LANESTOWN
1
Sunday Well
Bridge
LISSENHALL
GREAT
BALLYMADROUGH
Grave Yard
2
BALLYMADROUGH ROAD
HUTCHINSON'S STRAND
Big Marsh
Broad Meadow River
Green Field Bank
Horse
Marsh
SEAPOINT
ROAD COVERED BY HIGH TIDE
IRISH SEA
3
Gartan
Court
GARTAN DRIVE
DRIVE
PK
SEATOWN LANE
Lissen Hall
Seatown
Business Park
Prospect
Point
Seatown
Castle
GREENFIELDS
ESTUARY ROAD
A B C D E F
1
2
3
4
5
6
62
63
66
64
65
67
E
F

SEATOWN EAST
MOUNTGORRY
MALAHIDE ROAD
R106
Seamount View
St. Werburgh's Apts
Area Under Development
Tennis Ground
MOUNTGORRY WAY
FELTRIM ROAD
Feltrim Industrial Park
Blakeney House
Carwell Court
Damer House
Russell House
Plunket Hall
Ashe Court
Eyre Court
Waterside
Sports Ground
SEABURY GDNS
Church of the Sacred Heart
SEABURY AVE
SEABURY ROAD
CASTLE LAWNS
ESTUARY ROAD
CASTLE DOWNS RD
OLD YELLOW WALLS ROAD
LISSADEL WOOD
Chamley Park
KILLEEN AVENUE
KILLEEN CRES
To Malahide
Gainsborough
Talbot
Castleheath
Scoil an Duinninigh
Church of the Visitation (Cath)
ASPEN DR
ASPEN PK
ASPEN ROAD
BIRCHDALE RD
Kinsealy Court
ASHDALE ROAD
Kinsealy Shopping Centre
Melrose Park
Kinsealy Downs
Mount Drinan Park
Drynam Hall
DRYNAM DRIVE
DRYNAM AVENUE
DRYNAM CRESCENT
DRYNAM GROVE
DRYNAM RISE
KETTLES LANE
Holywell Crescent
Abington
AUBURN
DRINAN
Quarry
STREAMSTOWN LANE
FELTRIM
4
5
6

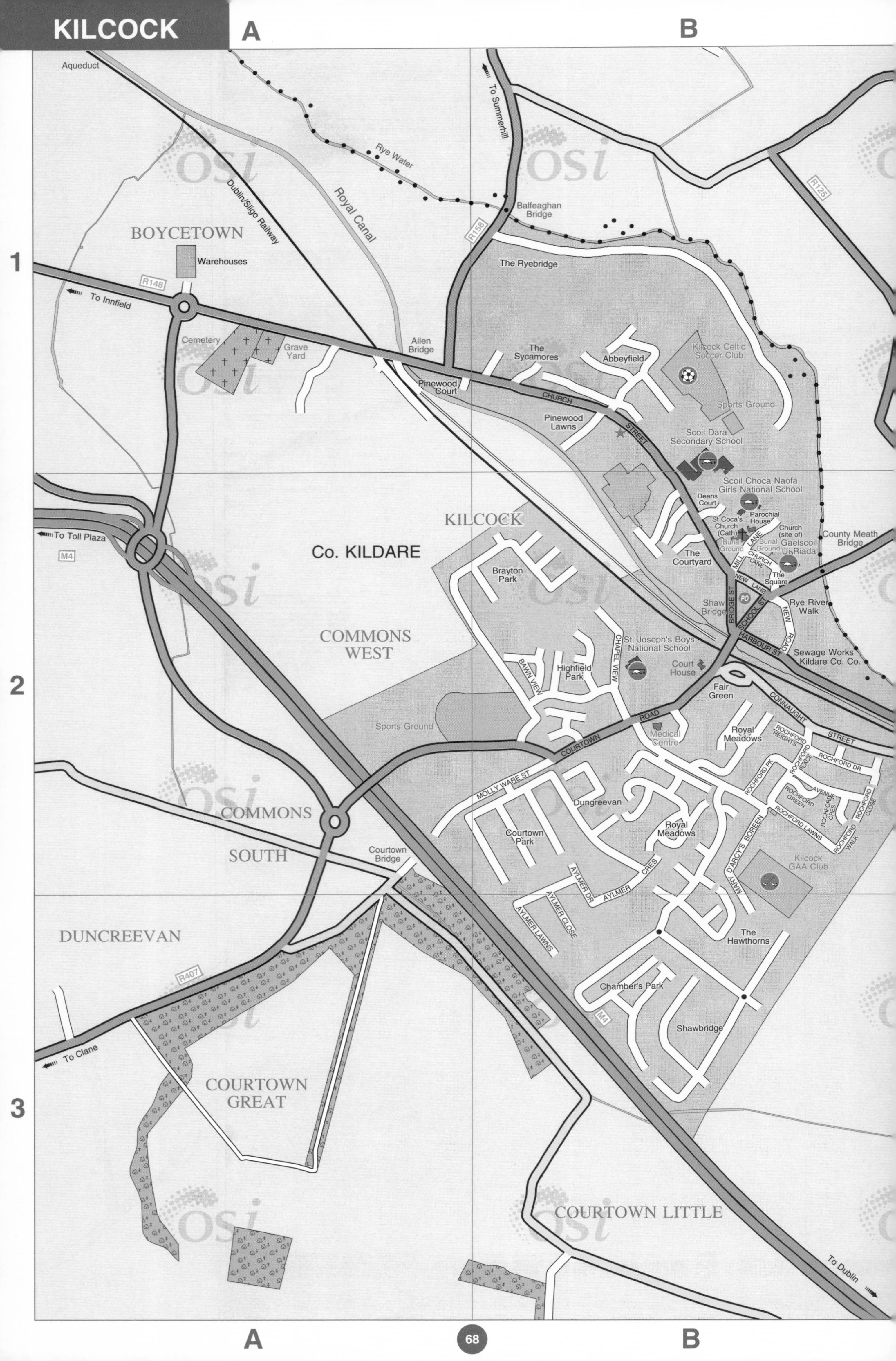
A
B
1
2
3
Aqueduct
To Summerhill
Rye Water
Royal Canal
Dublin/Sligo Railway
BOYCETOWN
Warehouses
R148
To Innfield
Balfeaghan Bridge
R158
R125
The Ryebridge
Cemetery
Grave Yard
Allen Bridge
Pinewood Court
The Sycamores
Abbeyfield
Kilcock Celtic Soccer Club
Sports Ground
CHURCH STREET
Pinewood Lawns
Scoil Dara Secondary School
Scoil Choca Naofa Girls National School
Deans Court
Parochial House
St Coca's Church (Cath)
Church (site of)
Gaelscoil Uí Riada
Burial Ground
MILL LANE
CHURCH LANE
The Courtyard
The Square
County Meath Bridge
KILCOCK
To Toll Plaza
M4
Co. KILDARE
Brayton Park
NEW LANE
BRIDGE ST
SCHOOL ST
PO
Shaw Bridge
Rye River Walk
NEW ROAD
HARBOUR ST
COMMONS WEST
St. Joseph's Boys National School
Sewage Works Kildare Co. Co.
BAWN VIEW
CHAPEL VIEW
Highfield Park
Court House
Fair Green
CONNAUGHT STREET
Sports Ground
COURTOWN ROAD
Medical Centre
Royal Meadows
ROCHFORD HEIGHTS
ROCHFORD PLACE
ROCHFORD DR
ROCHFORD PK
ROCHFORD AVENUE
ROCHFORD GREEN
ROCHFORD CRES
ROCHFORD CLOSE
ROCHFORD LAWNS
ROCHFORD WALK
MOLLY WARE ST
Dungreevan
COMMONS SOUTH
Courtown Park
Royal Meadows
MARY D'ARCY'S BOREEN
Kilcock GAA Club
Courtown Bridge
AYLMER DR
AYLMER CRES
AYLMER CLOSE
AYLMER LAWNS
The Hawthorns
DUNCREEVAN
R407
Chamber's Park
M4
Shawbridge
To Clane
COURTOWN GREAT
COURTOWN LITTLE
To Dublin

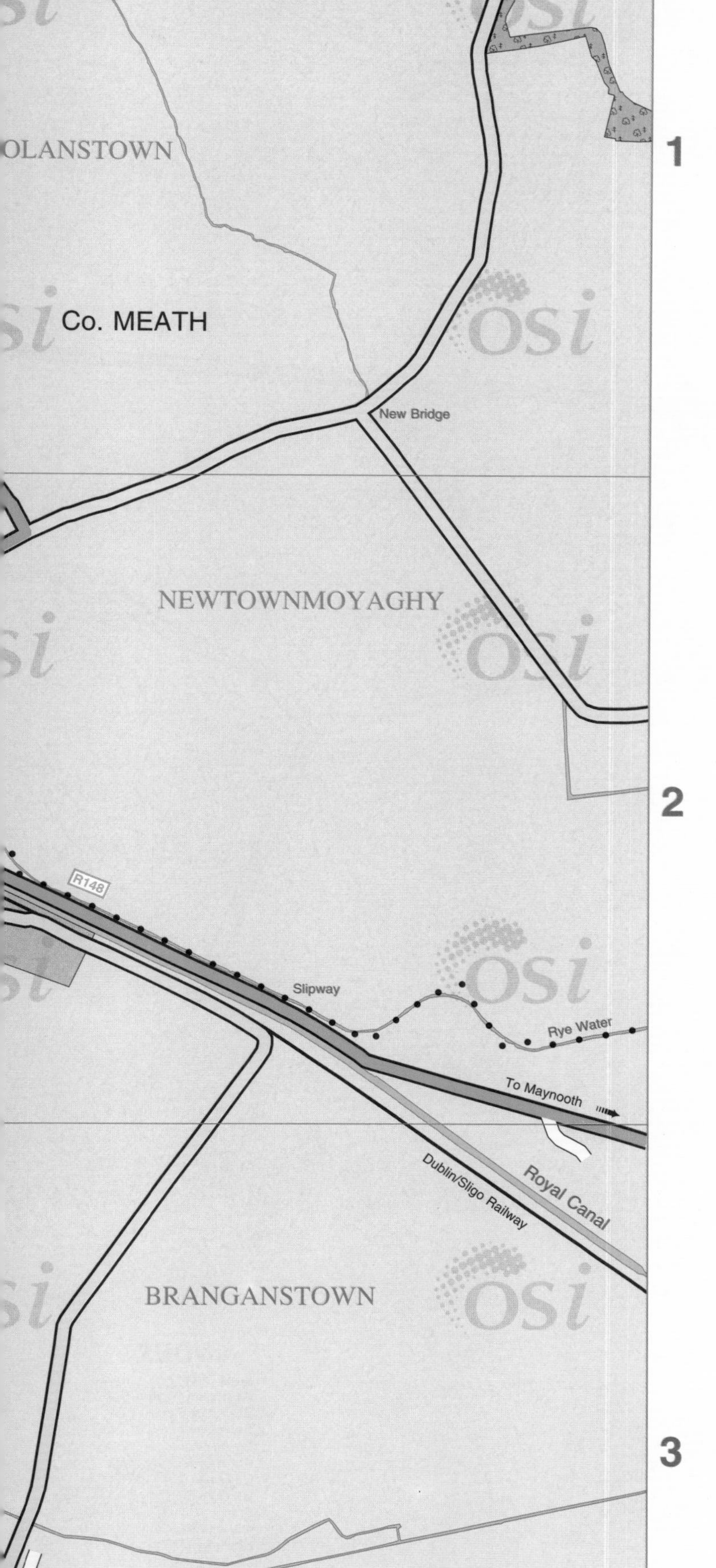

INDEX

Street	Grid	Street	Grid	Street	Grid
Abbeyfield	B1	Courtown Road	B2	Rochford Crescent	B2
Aylmer Close	B3	Deans Court	B2	Rochford Drive	B2
Allen Bridge	A1	Dungreevan	B2	Rochford Green	B2
Aylmer Crescent	B2	Fair Green	B2	Rochford Heights	B2
Aylmer Drive	B2	Harbour Street	B2	Rochford Lawns	B2
Aylmer Lawns	B3	Highfield Park	B2	Rochford Park	B2
Balfeaghan Bridge	B1	Mary D'Arcy's Boreen	B2	Rochford Place	B2
Bawn View	B2	Mill Lane	B2	Rochford Walk	B2
Brayton Park	A2	Molly Ware Street	B2	Royal Meadows	B2
Bridge Strret	B2	New Bridge	C1	School Street	B2
Chamber's Park	B3	New Lane	B2	Shawbridge	B3
Chapel View	B2	New Road	B2	The Courtyard	B2
Church Lane	B2	Pinewood Court	A1	The Hawthorns	B3
Church Street	B1	Pinewood Lawns	B1	The Ryebridge	B1
Connaught Street	B2	Rochford Avenue	B2	The Square	B2
Courtown Park	B2	Rochford Close	B2	The Sycamores	B1

PROSPEROUS

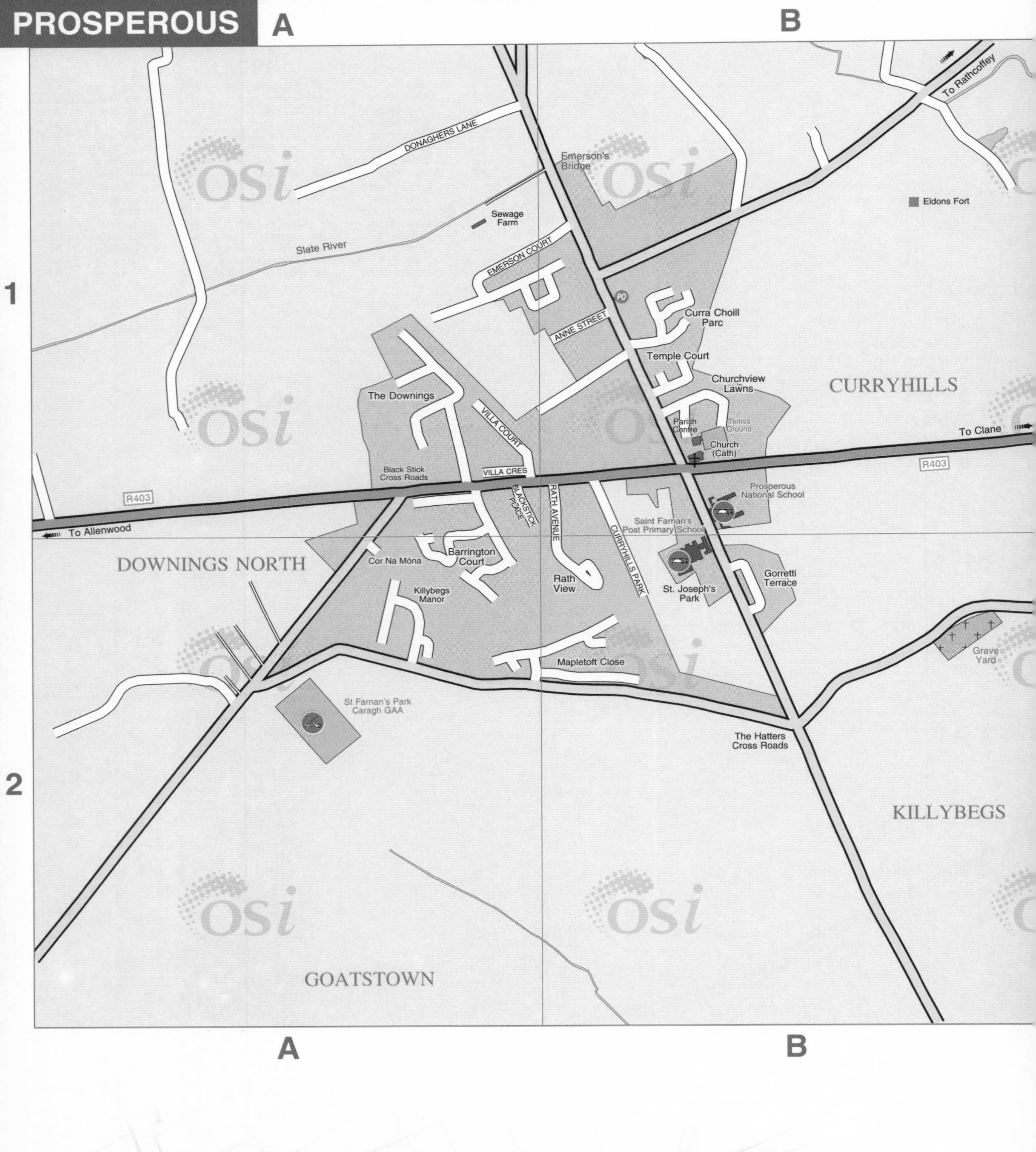

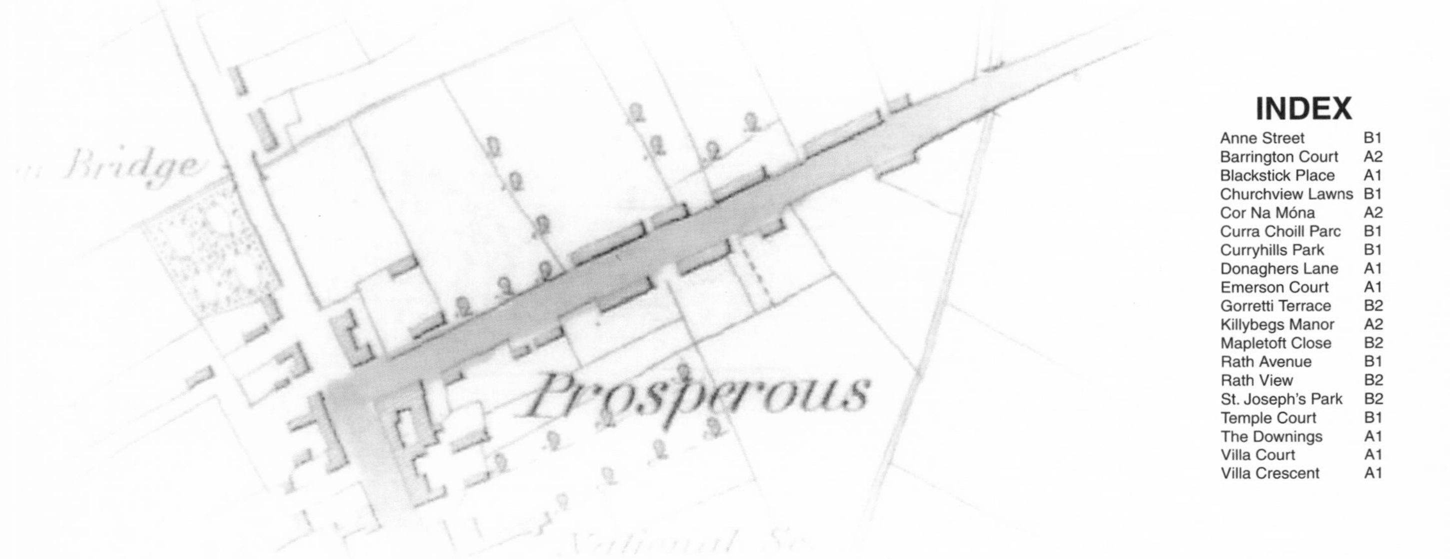

INDEX

Anne Street	B1
Barrington Court	A2
Blackstick Place	A1
Churchview Lawns	B1
Cor Na Móna	A2
Curra Choill Parc	B1
Curryhills Park	B1
Donaghers Lane	A1
Emerson Court	A1
Gorretti Terrace	B2
Killybegs Manor	A2
Mapletoft Close	B2
Rath Avenue	B1
Rath View	B2
St. Joseph's Park	B2
Temple Court	B1
The Downings	A1
Villa Court	A1
Villa Crescent	A1

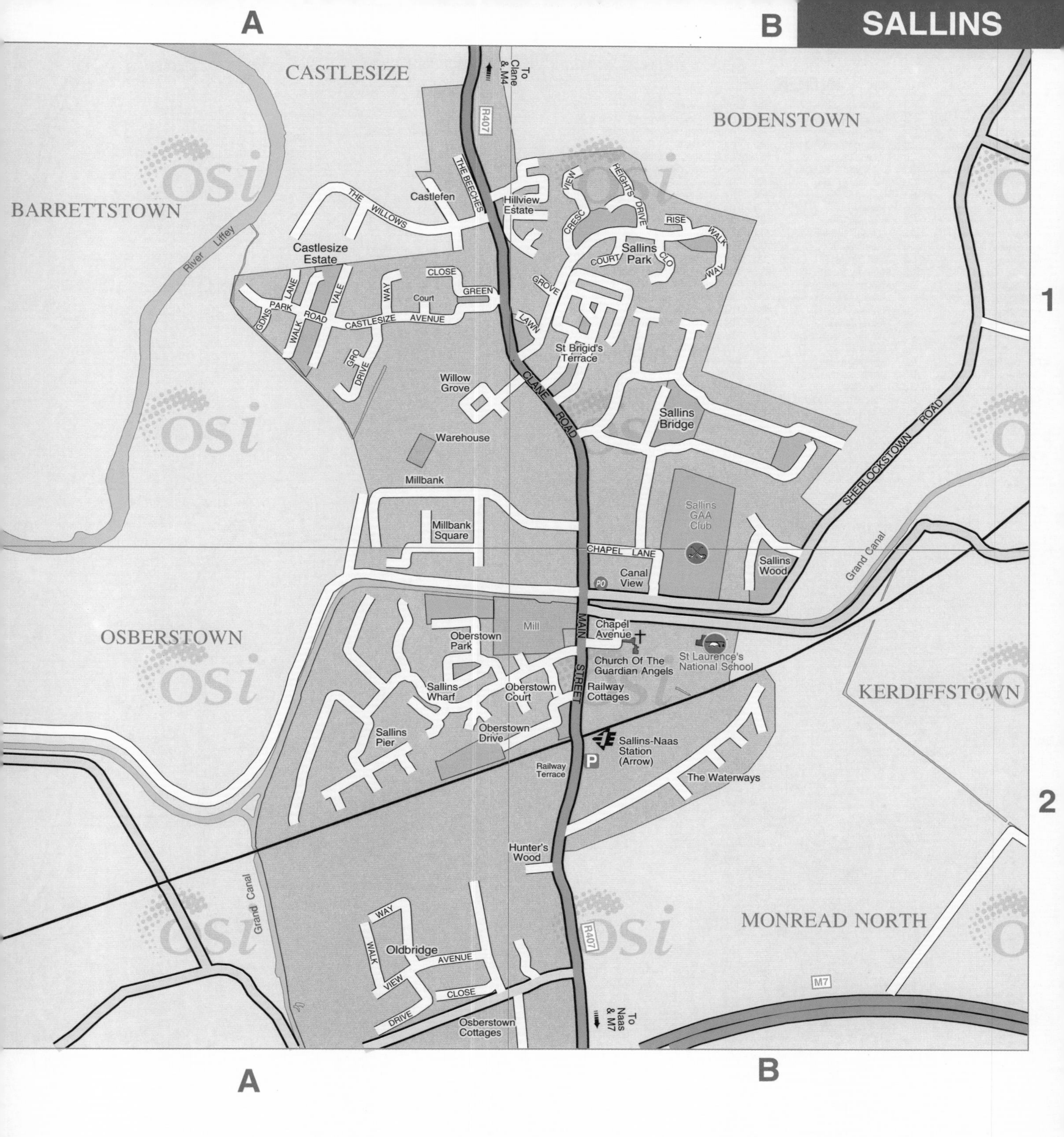

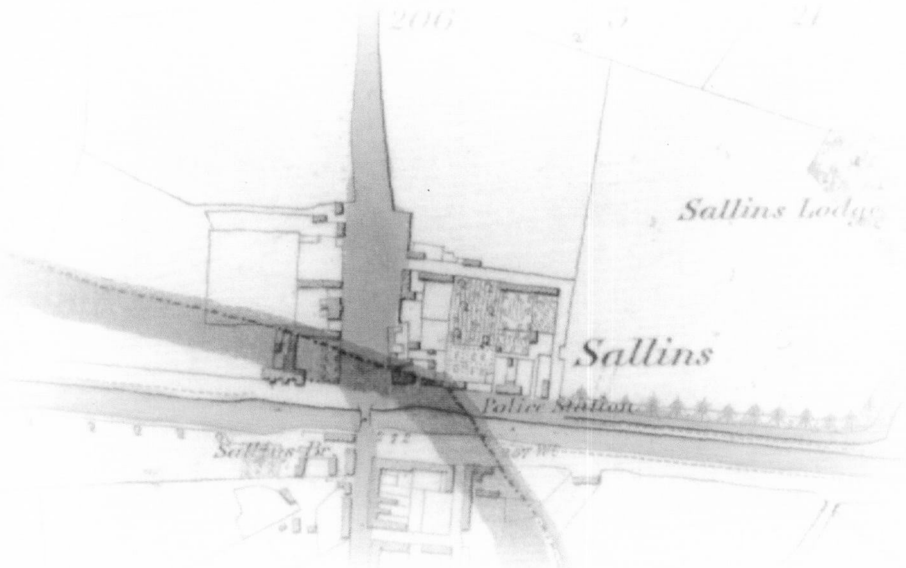

INDEX

Canal View	B2	Oldbridge View	A2
Castlefen	A1	Oldbridge Walk	A2
Castlesize Avenue	A1	Oldbridge Way	A2
Castlesize Close	A1	Railway Cottages	B2
Castlesize Drive	A1	Railway Terrace	B2
Castlesize Gardens	A1	Sallins Bridge	B1
Castlesize Green	A1	Sallins Park	B1
Castlesize Grove	A1	Sallins Park Close	B1
Castlesize Lane	A1	Sallins Park Court	B1
Castlesize Road	A1	Sallins Park Crescent	B1
Castlesize Vale	A1	Sallins Park Drive	B1
Castlesize Walk	A1	Sallins Park Grove	B1
Chapel Avenue	B2	Sallins Park Heights	B1
Chapel Lane	B1	Sallins Park Lawn	B1
Clane Road	B1	Sallins Park Rise	B1
Hillview Estate	B1	Sallins Park View	B1
Hunter's Wood	B2	Sallins Park Walk	B1
Main Street	B2	Sallins Park Way	B1
Millbank	A1	Sallins Pier	A2
Millbank Square	A1	Sallins Wharf	A2
Oberstown Cottages	A2	Sherlockstown Road	B1
Oberstown Court	B2	St Brigid's Terrace	B1
Oberstown Drive	B2	The Beeches	A1
Oberstown Park	A2	The Waterways	B2
Oldbridge Avenue	A2	The Willows	A1
Oldbridge Close	A2	Willow Grove	A1
Oldbridge Drive	A2		

INDEX

Abbey Court B3
Abbey Park Court C3
Abbey Park Glen C3
Abbey Park Green C3
Abbey Park Grove C3
Abbey Park Orchard C3
Abbey Park View C3
Abbeylands Apartments B3
Abbeylands Lodge C3
Alexandra Bridge C3
Alexandra Manor C3
Alexandra Walk C3
An Crochán B3
Ard Na Gappa A2
Ballingappa Road B2
Ballingappa Woods B2
Brooklands C2
Butterstream Drive A3
Butterstream Lawn A3
Capdoo Park B2
Central Park B3
Central Park Avenue B3
Central Park Way B3
Churchfield B3
Clonwood Heights A2
College Grove B3
College Road B2
College Road East B2
Collegewood Park A2
College Wood Manor A3
Dublin Road C2
Gollymochy Bridge B1
Halfmile Bridge A3
Higgins Lane B2
Hillview B3
Hillview Green B2
Hillview Heights B2
Liffey Lawns B3
Main Street B3
Meadow Court A2
Millicent Road B3
Motte B3
Oatfield Park B2
Otomy Close B3
Otomy Crescent B3
Otomy Drive B3
Otomy Grove B3
Otomy Lawns B3
Park View B3
Prosperous Road A3
Sallins Road B3
St. Brigid's Terrace B3
Sunday's Well B3
The Avenue, Collegewood Park A2
The Avenue, Hillview Heights B2
The Cloisters B3
The Close, Collegewood Park A2
The Close, Hillview Heights B2
The Crescent, Collegewood Pk A2
The Crescent, Hillview Heights B2
The Drive, Collegewood Park A2
The Drive, Hillview Heights A2
The Elms B2
The Green, Hillview Heights B2
The Grove, Collegewood Park A2
The Grove, Hillview Heights B2
The Lawn, Hillview Heights B2
The Lawns, Collegewood Park A2
The Meadows, Collegewood Pk A2
The Orchard, Hillview Heights B2
The Rise, Collegewood Park A2
The Rise, Hillview Heights B2
The Walk, Hillview Heights B2
Thompson Enterprise Centre B2
Yew Tree Square B3

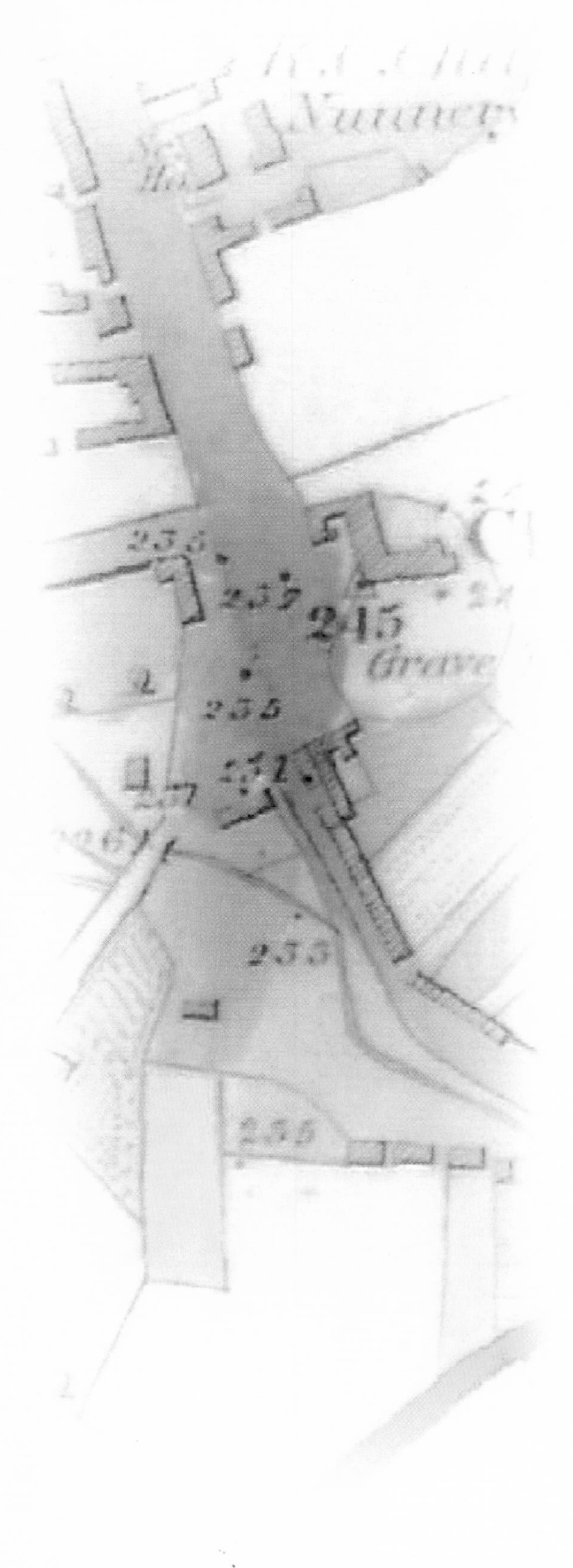

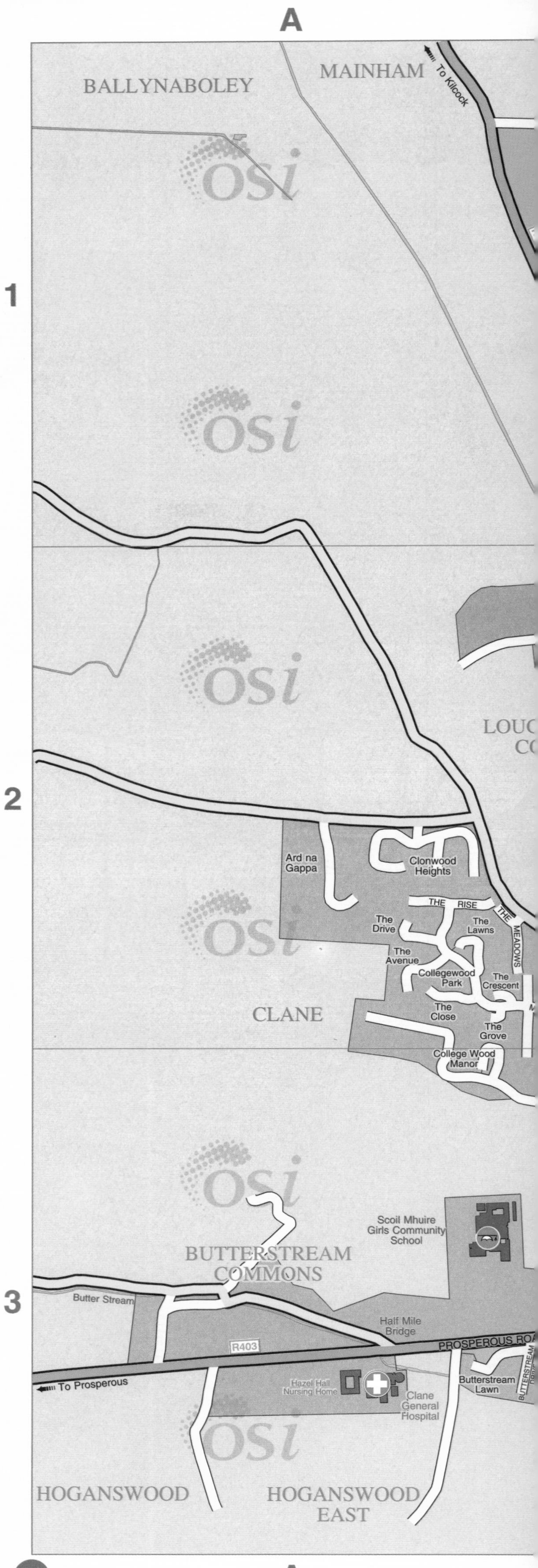

B
C
CASTLEBROWN or CLONGOWES
Clongowes Wood College
Chapel
Sports Grounds
RICHARDSTOWN
Golf Club
1
The Pale Ditch
Gollymochy Bridge
Gollymochy River
siness Park
HIGGINS LANE
To Celbridge
Thompson
erprise Centre
COLLEGE ROAD
R403
OLLARD
MONS
The Lawn
The Cresent
The Grove
THE AVENUE
THE ORCHARD
The Close
2
The Green
THE
College Road East
THE RISE
CAPDOO
Ballinagappa Woods
THE DRIVE
The Walk
DUBLIN ROAD
Hillview Green
Hillview Heights
Capdoo Park
CAPDOO COMMONS
Brooklands
COURT
OATFIELD
ROAD
The Elms
COLLEGE GROVE
St Brigid's Terrace
PARK
River Liffey
St.Brigid's Spring
Hillview
VIEW
Sports Ground
LAWNS
Otomy Estate
Adult Education Centre
The Cloisters
CLOSE
DRIVE
GLEN
CENTRAL PARK
Abbey Park
Abbeylands Apartments
GRO
CRES
LIFFEY
Health Centre
St Patrick's & St Brigid's Church (Cath)
GREEN
GROVE
Sports Ground
MAIN STREET
LAWNS
AVENUE
CENTRAL PARK
Burial Ground
ORCHARD
Scoil Bhríde Girls National School
Abbeylands Lodge
3
Site of Monastery
CENTRAL PARK WAY
COURT
Abbey Court
Churchfield
Grave Yard
Club House
Yew Tree Square
Clane Abbey (in ruins)
ABBEYLAND
Alexandra Walk
Clane GAA Club
Bullán
PARK VIEW
ROAD
Alexandra Manor
ROCKAUN
COMMONS
Base of Stone Cross (Wart Stone)
R407
SALLINS
An Crochán
MILLICENT
Motte
Sunday's Well
ROAD
To Sallins
Alexandra Bridge
B
C

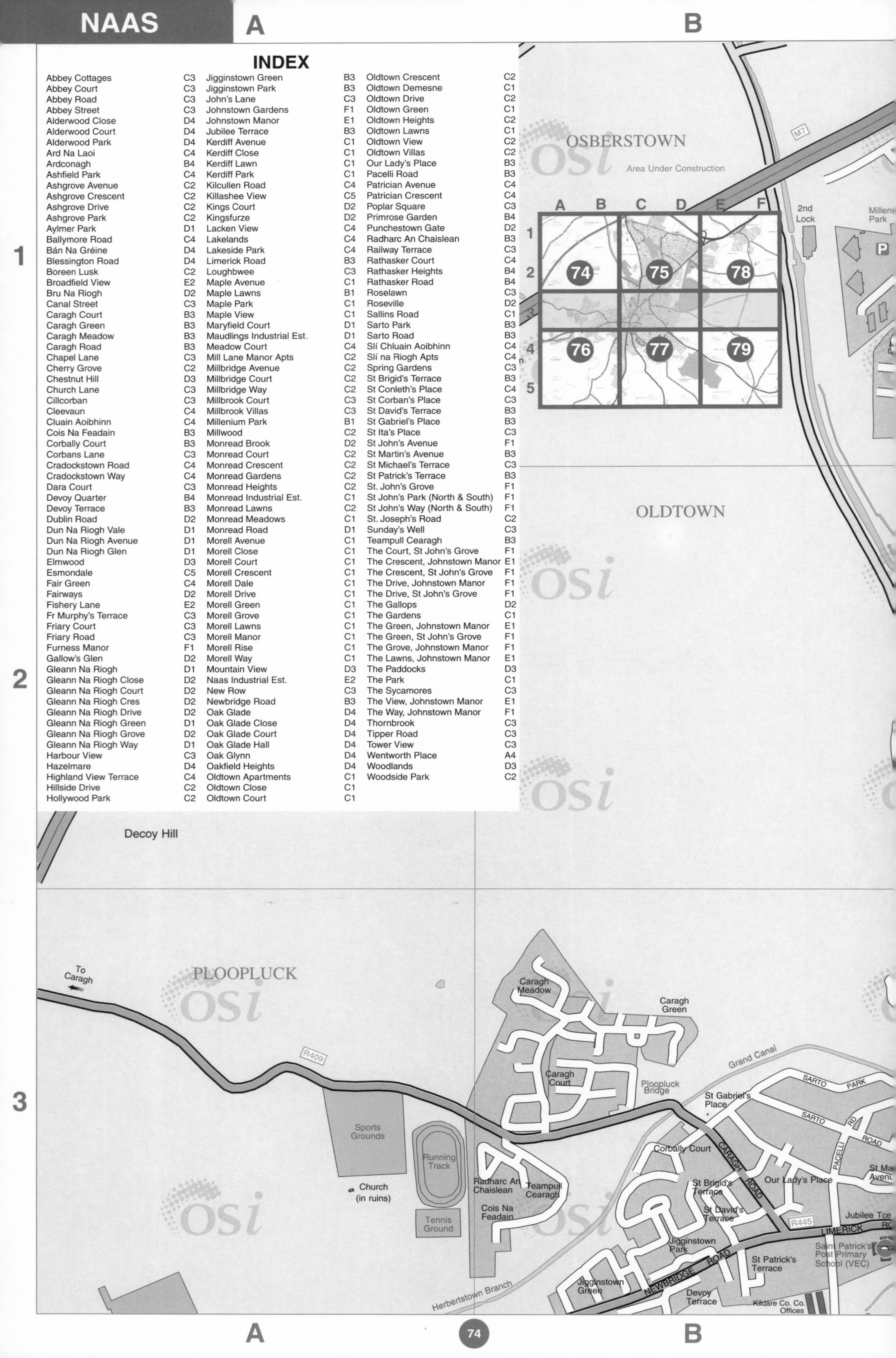

INDEX

Street	Grid
Abbey Cottages	C3
Abbey Court	C3
Abbey Road	C3
Abbey Street	C3
Alderwood Close	D4
Alderwood Court	D4
Alderwood Park	D4
Ard Na Laoi	C4
Ardconagh	B4
Ashfield Park	C4
Ashgrove Avenue	C2
Ashgrove Crescent	C2
Ashgrove Drive	C2
Ashgrove Park	C2
Aylmer Park	D1
Ballymore Road	C4
Bán Na Gréine	D4
Blessington Road	D4
Boreen Lusk	C2
Broadfield View	E2
Bru Na Riogh	D2
Canal Street	C3
Caragh Court	B3
Caragh Green	B3
Caragh Meadow	B3
Caragh Road	B3
Chapel Lane	C3
Cherry Grove	C2
Chestnut Hill	D3
Church Lane	C3
Cillcorban	C3
Cleevaun	C4
Cluain Aoibhinn	C4
Cois Na Feadain	B3
Corbally Court	B3
Corbans Lane	C3
Cradockstown Road	C4
Cradockstown Way	C4
Dara Court	C3
Devoy Quarter	B4
Devoy Terrace	B3
Dublin Road	D2
Dun Na Riogh Vale	D1
Dun Na Riogh Avenue	D1
Dun Na Riogh Glen	D1
Elmwood	D3
Esmondale	C5
Fair Green	C4
Fairways	D2
Fishery Lane	E2
Fr Murphy's Terrace	C3
Friary Court	C3
Friary Road	C3
Furness Manor	F1
Gallow's Glen	D2
Gleann Na Riogh	D1
Gleann Na Riogh Close	D2
Gleann Na Riogh Court	D2
Gleann Na Riogh Cres	D2
Gleann Na Riogh Drive	D2
Gleann Na Riogh Green	D1
Gleann Na Riogh Grove	D2
Gleann Na Riogh Way	D1
Harbour View	C3
Hazelmare	D4
Highland View Terrace	C4
Hillside Drive	C2
Hollywood Park	C2
Jigginstown Green	B3
Jigginstown Park	B3
John's Lane	C3
Johnstown Gardens	F1
Johnstown Manor	E1
Jubilee Terrace	B3
Kerdiff Avenue	C1
Kerdiff Close	C1
Kerdiff Lawn	C1
Kerdiff Park	C1
Kilcullen Road	C4
Killashee View	C5
Kings Court	D2
Kingsfurze	D2
Lacken View	C4
Lakelands	C4
Lakeside Park	C4
Limerick Road	B3
Loughbwee	C3
Maple Avenue	C1
Maple Lawns	B1
Maple Park	C1
Maple View	C1
Maryfield Court	D1
Maudlings Industrial Est.	D1
Meadow Court	C4
Mill Lane Manor Apts	C2
Millbridge Avenue	C2
Millbridge Court	C2
Millbridge Way	C2
Millbrook Court	C3
Millbrook Villas	C3
Millenium Park	B1
Millwood	C2
Monread Brook	D2
Monread Court	C2
Monread Crescent	C2
Monread Gardens	C2
Monread Heights	C2
Monread Industrial Est.	C1
Monread Lawns	C2
Monread Meadows	C1
Monread Road	D1
Morell Avenue	C1
Morell Close	C1
Morell Court	C1
Morell Crescent	C1
Morell Dale	C1
Morell Drive	C1
Morell Green	C1
Morell Grove	C1
Morell Lawns	C1
Morell Manor	C1
Morell Rise	C1
Morell Way	C1
Mountain View	D3
Naas Industrial Est.	E2
New Row	C3
Newbridge Road	B3
Oak Glade	D4
Oak Glade Close	D4
Oak Glade Court	D4
Oak Glade Hall	D4
Oak Glynn	D4
Oakfield Heights	D4
Oldtown Apartments	C1
Oldtown Close	C1
Oldtown Court	C1
Oldtown Crescent	C2
Oldtown Demesne	C1
Oldtown Drive	C2
Oldtown Green	C1
Oldtown Heights	C2
Oldtown Lawns	C1
Oldtown View	C2
Oldtown Villas	C2
Our Lady's Place	B3
Pacelli Road	B3
Patrician Avenue	C4
Patrician Crescent	C4
Poplar Square	C3
Primrose Garden	B4
Punchestown Gate	D2
Radharc An Chaislean	B3
Railway Terrace	C3
Rathasker Court	C4
Rathasker Heights	B4
Rathasker Road	B4
Roselawn	C3
Roseville	D2
Sallins Road	C1
Sarto Park	B3
Sarto Road	B3
Slí Chluain Aoibhinn	C4
Slí na Riogh Apts	C4
Spring Gardens	C3
St Brigid's Terrace	B3
St Conleth's Place	C4
St Corban's Place	C3
St David's Terrace	B3
St Gabriel's Place	B3
St Ita's Place	C3
St John's Avenue	F1
St Martin's Avenue	B3
St Michael's Terrace	C3
St Patrick's Terrace	B3
St. John's Grove	F1
St John's Park (North & South)	F1
St John's Way (North & South)	F1
St. Joseph's Road	C2
Sunday's Well	C3
Teampull Cearagh	B3
The Court, St John's Grove	F1
The Crescent, Johnstown Manor	E1
The Crescent, St John's Grove	F1
The Drive, Johnstown Manor	F1
The Drive, St John's Grove	F1
The Gallops	D2
The Gardens	C1
The Green, Johnstown Manor	E1
The Green, St John's Grove	F1
The Grove, Johnstown Manor	F1
The Lawns, Johnstown Manor	E1
The Paddocks	D3
The Park	C1
The Sycamores	C3
The View, Johnstown Manor	E1
The Way, Johnstown Manor	F1
Thornbrook	C3
Tipper Road	C3
Tower View	C3
Wentworth Place	A4
Woodlands	D3
Woodside Park	C2

C
D
1
2
3
Monread Industrial Estate
Area Under Construction
Larchfield Park Nursing Home
Maryfield Court
MONREAD ROAD
MORELL LAWNS
Morell Green
MORELL CLOSE
MORELL COURT
MORELL RISE
MORELL WAY
MONREAD MEADOWS
Morell Avenue
Morell Grove
Morell Manor
Morell Crescent
Morell Dale
MORELL DRIVE
SALLINS ROAD
To Sallins & Train Station
Kerdiff Park
Kerdiff Avenue
Kerdiff Close
Kerdiff Lawn
The Gardens
Oldtown Green
Oldtown Court
Aylmer Park
Globe Retail Park
Maudlings Industrial Estate
Dún Na Ríogh
GLEN
VALE
AVENUE
GREEN
WAY
COURT
CLOSE
CRESCENT
DRIVE
Gleann Na Ríogh
Gleann Na Ríogh Grove
MAPLE PARK
MAPLE AVENUE
Under Construction
Oldtown Demesne
Oldtown Apartments
Oldtown Lawns
The Park
OLDTOWN DEMESNE
Playground
Close
Drive
Crescent
Oldtown Estate
Villas
Heights
View
Cherry Grove
Hillside Drive
Scoil Bhride National School
Naas GAA Club
Octagon Pond
Monread Lawns
Monread Gardens
Monread Brook
Bru na Riogh
Roseville
Monread Court
Monread Heights
Monread Crescent
Fairways
Roseville
Club House
Sports Ground
Cemetery
The Gallops
Greenaun
St Corban's Cemetery
Tennis Grounds
Woodside Park
BOREEN LUSK
ASHGROVE
ASHGROVE PARK
AVENUE
CRESCENT
ASHGROVE DRIVE
DUBLIN ROAD
MONREAD AVENUE
Kings Court
Punchestown Gate
Kingsfurze
Playground
Gallow's Glen
Mill Lane Manor Apts
Millwood
4th Lock
ST JOSEPH'S ROAD
MILLBRIDGE AVENUE
MILLBRIDGE WAY
COURT
5th Lock
Hollywood Park
St Corban's Place
The Sycamores
Spring Gardens
Victoria Terrace
Railway Terrace
Naas Convent National School
Saint David's National School
Fr Murphy's Terrace
Abbey Court
St Mary's Secondary College (Girls)
Church Of Our Lady & Saint David (Cath)
CHAPEL LANE
Poplar Square
Woodlands
Roselawn
Stand
Naas Racecourse
TIPPER ROAD
Thornbrook
I.D.A. Ireland
Chestnut Hill
ABBEY ROAD
Town Hall
JOHN'S LANE
Friary Court
Monastery
Saint David's Church (C of I)
FRIARY ROAD
BLESSINGTON ROAD
Health Centre
ABBEY STREET
CHURCH LANE
Factory
Millbrook Court
Millbrook Villas
Elmwood
The Paddocks
CANAL STREET
MAIN STREET
Harbour View
Cillcorban
CORBAN'S LANE
C.B.S. Secondary School
NEW ROW
Dara Court
Loughbwee
Scoil Corban
Lakelands
Sunday's Well
Naas Mail Centre
Mountain View
St Michael's Terrace
Tower View
Swimming Pool
Sunday's Well
TIPPER WEST
R407
R445
R410
M7
osi

A
B
3
4
5
To Caragh
PLOOPLUCK
R409
Caragh Meadow
Caragh Green
Caragh Court
Plooppluck Bridge
Grand Canal
SARTO PARK
SARTO ROAD
St Gabriel's Place
Sports Grounds
Running Track
Corbally Court
CARAGH ROAD
PACELLI RD
Church (in ruins)
Radharc An Chaislean
Teampull Cearagh
St Brigid's Terrace
Our Lady's Place
St Ma Avenu
Tennis Ground
Cois Na Feadain
St David's Terrace
R445
Jubilee Tce
LIMERICK
Jigginstown Park
Saint Patrick's Post Primary School (VEC)
NEWBRIDGE ROAD
St Patrick's Terrace
Herbertstown Branch
Jigginstown Green
Devoy Terrace
Kildare Co. Co. Offices
Ardconagh
Jigginstown Bridge
Jigginstown Castle (In Ruins)
Jigginstown Commercial Centre
Devoy Quarter
R445
Grand Canal
To Newbridge
Wentworth Place
Area Under Construction
Primrose Garden
Area Under Construction
Limerick Bridge
RATHASKER
Rathas Heights
Canal Supply
JIGGINSTOWN
Broad View
BLUEBELL
Spring
R448
To Kilcullen & Brannockstown

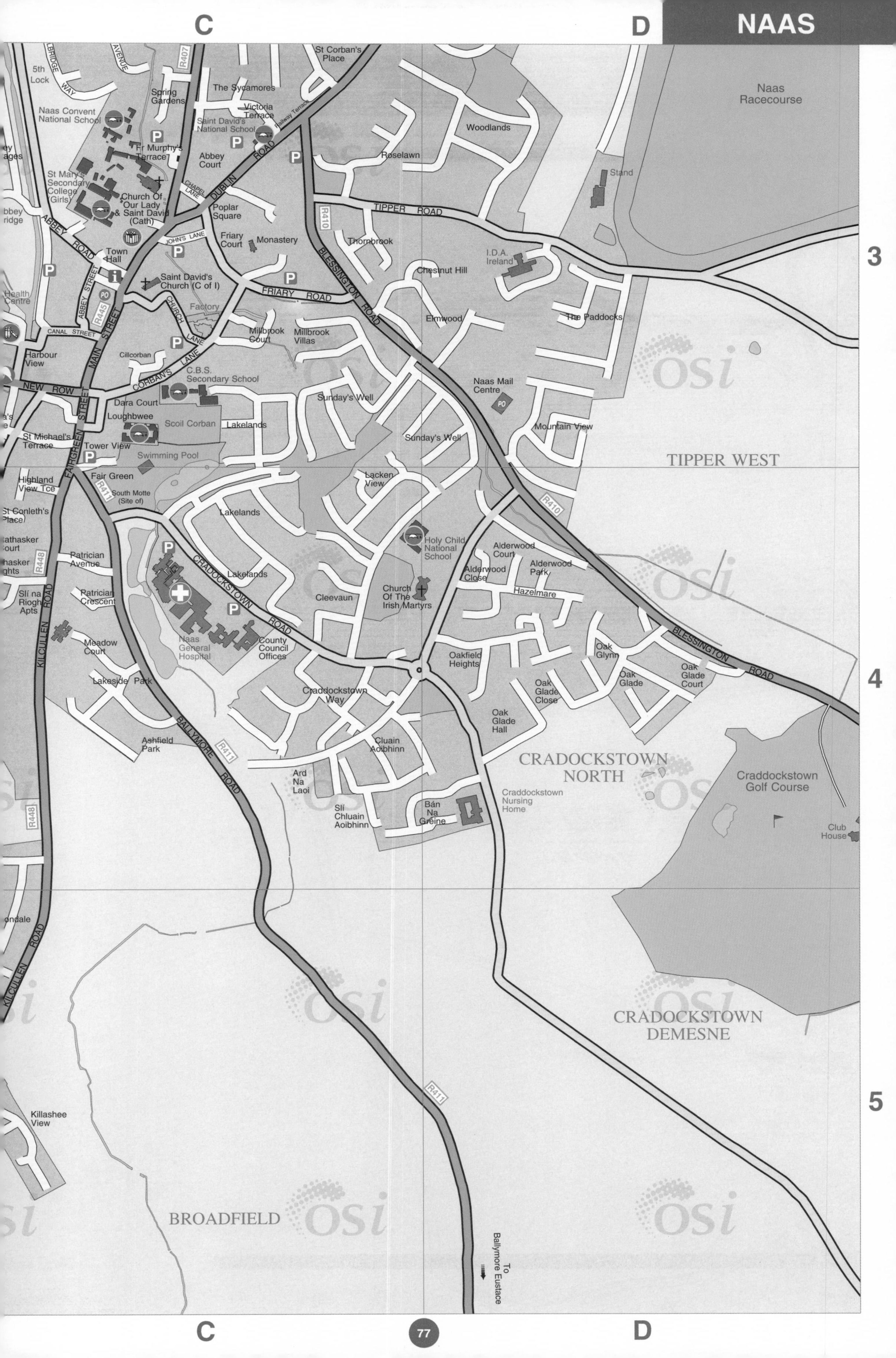
C
D
5th Lock
Spring Gardens
The Sycamores
St Corban's Place
Naas Convent National School
Saint David's National School
Victoria Terrace
Fr Murphy's Terrace
Abbey Court
Roselawn
Woodlands
Naas Racecourse
Stand
St Mary's Secondary College (Girls)
Church Of Our Lady & Saint David (Cath)
Poplar Square
DUBLIN ROAD
TIPPER ROAD
R410
Thornbrook
Friary Court
Monastery
I.D.A. Ireland
ABBEY ROAD
Town Hall
JOHN'S LANE
Chestnut Hill
Saint David's Church (C of I)
FRIARY ROAD
BLESSINGTON ROAD
Elmwood
The Paddocks
Factory
CHURCH LANE
ABBEY STREET
MAIN STREET
R445
CANAL STREET
Millbrook Court
Millbrook Villas
Harbour View
Cillcorban
CORBAN'S LANE
C.B.S. Secondary School
Naas Mail Centre
NEW ROW
Dara Court
Sunday's Well
Loughbwee
Scoil Corban
Lakelands
Mountain View
St Michael's Terrace
FAIRGREEN STREET
Tower View
Swimming Pool
Sunday's Well
TIPPER WEST
Highland View Tce
Fair Green
Lacken View
R411
South Motte (Site of)
St Conleth's Place
Lakelands
Holy Child National School
Alderwood Court
Alderwood Park
Alderwood Close
Hazelmare
Patrician Avenue
R448
Lakelands
CRADOCKSTOWN ROAD
Patrician Crescent
Cleevaun
Church Of The Irish Martyrs
Slí na Riogh Apts
KILCULLEN ROAD
Meadow Court
Naas General Hospital
County Council Offices
Oakfield Heights
Oak Glynn
Oak Glade
Oak Glade Court
Lakeside Park
Craddockstown Way
Oak Glade Close
Oak Glade Hall
Ashfield Park
BALLYMORE ROAD
Cluain Aoibhinn
CRADOCKSTOWN NORTH
Craddockstown Golf Course
Ard Na Laoi
Craddockstown Nursing Home
Slí Chluain Aoibhinn
Bán Na Gréine
Club House
CRADOCKSTOWN DEMESNE
Killashee View
BROADFIELD
To Ballymore Eustace
3
4
5
C
D

E
F
To Dublin & M50
Tobenavoher Bridge
N7
PALMERSTOWN
Maudlings Interchange
Grave Yard
Church (in ruins)
THE GREEN
THE DRIVE
CRESCENT
St John's Park (North)
TOBERTON
St John's Way (North)
SAINT JOHN'S AVENUE
Saint John's Grove
St John's Park (South)
THE COURT
St John's Way (South)
THE VIEW
Johnstown Gardens
THE LAWNS
THE DRIVE
THE WAY
THE GROVE
Johnstown Manor
THE CRESCENT
THE GREEN
Morell River
Industrial Estate
Furness Manor
Naas Industrial Estate
JOHNSTOWN
WESTOWN
Irish Equine Centre
FISHERY LANE
Aqueduct
KINGSFURZE
Chur (in rui
Morell Bridge
TIPPER NORTH
TIPPER EAST
A B C D E F
1 2 3 4 5
74 75 78
76 77 79

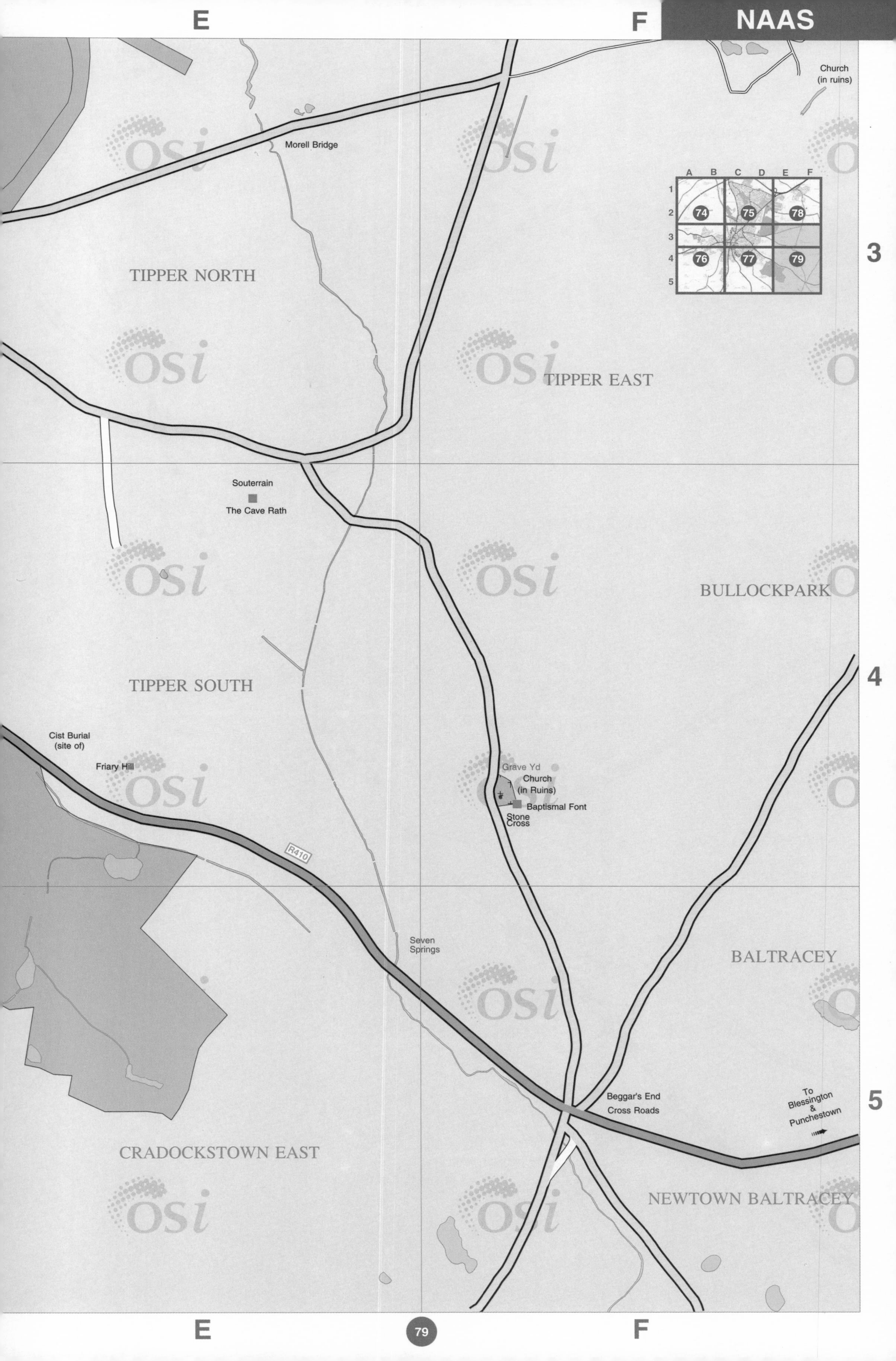
E
F
Church
(in ruins)
Morell Bridge
A B C D E F
1
2
3
4
5
74
75
78
76
77
79
3
TIPPER NORTH
TIPPER EAST
Souterrain
The Cave Rath
BULLOCKPARK
4
TIPPER SOUTH
Cist Burial
(site of)
Friary Hill
Grave Yd
Church
(in Ruins)
Baptismal Font
Stone
Cross
R410
Seven
Springs
BALTRACEY
Beggar's End
Cross Roads
To
Blessington
&
Punchestown
5
CRADOCKSTOWN EAST
NEWTOWN BALTRACEY
E
F

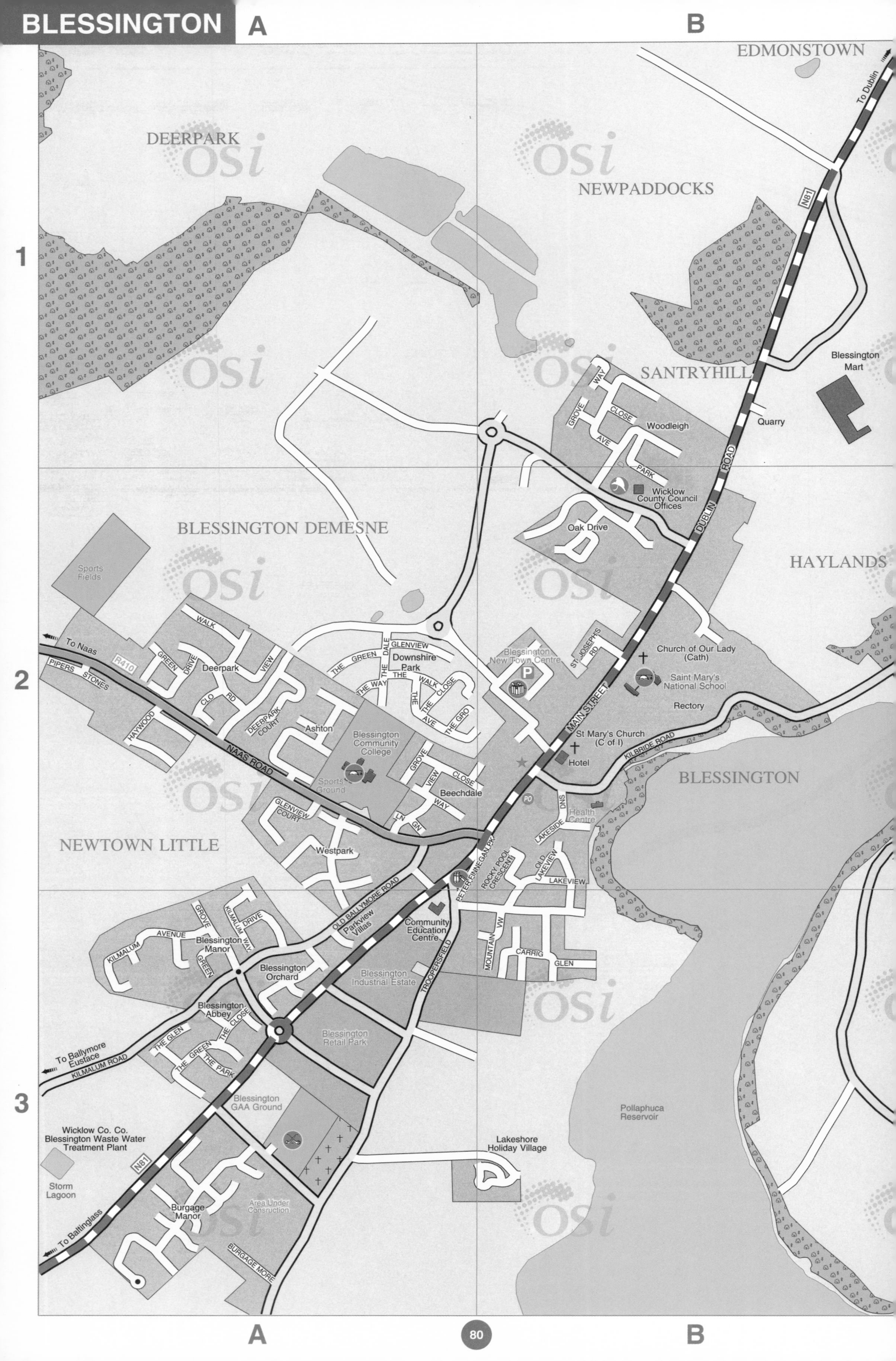
A
B
1
2
3
EDMONSTOWN
To Dublin
DEERPARK
NEWPADDOCKS
N81
SANTRYHILL
Blessington Mart
Quarry
Woodleigh
GROVE
WAY
CLOSE
AVE
PARK
Wicklow County Council Offices
DUBLIN ROAD
Oak Drive
BLESSINGTON DEMESNE
HAYLANDS
Sports Fields
To Naas
R410
PIPERS STONES
HAYWOOD
GREEN
DRIVE
WALK
VIEW
Deerpark
CLO
RD
DEERPARK COURT
NAAS ROAD
Ashton
THE GREEN
THE DALE
GLENVIEW
Downshire Park
THE WAY
THE
WALK
CLOSE
THE AVE
THE GRO
Blessington Community College
Sports Ground
Blessington New Town Centre
ST JOSEPH'S RD
MAIN STREET
Church of Our Lady (Cath)
Saint Mary's National School
Rectory
St Mary's Church (C of I)
Hotel
KILBRIDE ROAD
BLESSINGTON
GROVE
VIEW
CLOSE
Beechdale
WAY
LN
GN
GLENVIEW COURT
Westpark
NEWTOWN LITTLE
PO
DNS
LAKESIDE
Health Centre
PETER FINNEGAN PK
ROCKY POOL CRESCENT
OLD LAKEVIEW
LAKEVIEW
OLD BALLYMORE ROAD
Parkview Villas
Community Education Centre
GROVE
KILMALUM WAY
DRIVE
AVENUE
KILMALUM
Blessington Manor
GREEN
Blessington Orchard
Blessington Industrial Estate
TROOPERSFIELD
MOUNTAIN VW
CARRIG
GLEN
Blessington Abbey
THE CLOSE
THE GLEN
THE GREEN
THE PARK
Blessington Retail Park
To Ballymore Eustace
KILMALUM ROAD
Blessington GAA Ground
Pollaphuca Reservoir
Wicklow Co. Co. Blessington Waste Water Treatment Plant
Storm Lagoon
N81
Lakeshore Holiday Village
Burgage Manor
Area Under Consruction
BURGAGE MORE
To Baltinglass

C

CROSSCOOLHARBOUR

RED LANE

Tír na Nóg Montossori School

HOLYVALLEY

Blessington Bridge

P

Rundle Bridge

KNOCKIERAN LOWER

KNOCKIERAN UPPER

1

2

3

C

INDEX

Ashton A2
Beechdale Close A2
Beechdale Garden A2
Beechdale Grove A2
Beechdale Lawn A2
Beechdale View A2
Beechdale Way A2
Blessington Abbey A3
Blessington Bridge C2
Blessington Ind. Estate A3
Blessington Manor A3
Blessington Orchard A3
Burgage Manor A3
Burgage More A3
Carrig Glen B3
Deerpark Close A2
Deerpark Court A2
Deerpark Drive A2
Deerpark Green A2
Deerpark Road A2
Deerpark View A2
Deerpark Walk A2
Downshire Park The Avenue A2
Downshire Park The Close A2
Downshire Park The Dale A2
Downshire Park The Green A2
Downshire Park The Grove A2
Downshire Park The Walk A2
Downshire Park The Walk A2
Downshire Park The Way A2
Glenview Court A2
Kilmalum Drive A3
Kilmalum Green A3
Kilmalum Grove A3
Kilmalum Avenue A3
Kilmalum Road A3
Kilmalum Way A3
Kilbride Road B2
Lakeshore Holiday Village B3
Lakeside Downs B2
Lakeview B2
Main Street B2
Mountain View B3
Naas Road A2
Oak Drive B2
Old Ballymore Road A3
Old Lakeview B2
Parkview Villas A3
Peter Finnegan Park B2
Pipers Stones A2
Red Lane C1
Rocky Pool Crescent B2
St. Joseph's Road B2
The Close A3
The Glen A3
The Green A3
The Park A3
Troopersfield A3
Westpark A2
Woodleigh Avenue B1
Woodleigh Close B1
Woodleigh Grove B1
Woodleigh Park B1
Woodleigh Way B1

Mart Ho.

Hotel

School H

BELMONT
DEMESNE
TEMPLECARRIG
LOWER
COOLAGAD
KINDLESTOWN UPPER
To
Bray
R761
Grave
Yard
Rathdown Castle
(Site of)
Saint
Crispins
Church
(In Ruins)
Redford
Sports Gr
Redford
Court
RATHDOWN
ROAD
SEA VIEW
Redford Park
Willowmere
RISE
REDFORD
Blacklion
Manor
Rathdown Park
La Touche
Park
Willow
Bank
Saint Killian's
RC Church
Rathdown
Lawn
R762
RATHDOWN ROAD
Rathdown
Court
Saint Kev
National S
St Bridget's
Park
Oaklands
Court
Oaklands
CHURCH
Chapel
View
APPLEWOOD DRIVE
Applewood
Heights
CHAPEL ROAD
Lower Grattan
Park
Upper Grattan Park
Beechbrook
Park
RIVENDELL GROVE
Kindlestown Park
Kindlestown
Rise
Dromont
Kenmare Heights
Bellevue
Heights
KINDLESTOWN LOWER
Saint Laurence's
School
Kindlestown
Castle
(In Ruins)
Kindlestown
Heights
Greystones
Golf Course
Club H
The Poplars
Delgany Glen
The Nurseries
Burnaby Heights
CHAPEL
Carraig
Orchard
Castle
(In Ruins)
Castlefield T
Riverfield
Hillcrest
Ave
Priory
Way
Priory
Rise
Cherry
Orchard
Castle Villas
Meadow
Court
Bellevue
Cottages
Orchard
View
Adare Close
St Mary's
Church (RC)
Bellevue
Lawns
Carrick Villas
1
2
3

INDEX (GREYSTONES, DELGANY)

Adare Close C3
Applewood Drive C2
Applewood Heights C2
Ballydonagh Lane A2
Bayswater Terrace D2
Beechbrook Park C3
Bellevue Cottages B3
Bellevue Heights C3
Bellevue Lawns B3
Bellevue Park D2
Bellevue Road D2
Blackberry Lane B4
Blacklion Manor C2
Burnaby Avenue D4
Burnaby Court D4
Burnaby Heights C3
Burnaby Lawns D4
Burnaby Manor D2
Burnaby Mews D2
Burnaby Mill D4
Burnaby Park D3
Burnaby Road D3
Burnaby Woods D3
Carraig Orchard C3
Carrick Villas C3
Carrig Villas C4
Castle Villas C3
Castlefield Terrace C3
Chapel Road C2
Chapel View C2
Charlesland Court D4
Charlesland Park D4
Charlesland Wood D4
Cherry Orchard C3
Church Gate D2
Church Lane C2
Church Road D2
Cliff Road D2
Convent Court B4
Delgany Glen C3
Delgany Park C4
Delgany Wood C4
Dromont B3
Eden Road D2
Elsinore C4
Erskine Avenue D3
Fair Green A4
Fairfield Park D2
Fairways D4
Glen of the Downs A4
Glenbrook Park C4
Harbour Court D2
Hawkins Lane D3
Hethervue D2
Hillcrest Avenue C3
Hillside D2
Hillside Road D2
Kenmare Heights C3
Killincarrick Road D2
Kimberley Court D2
Kimberley Road D2
Kindlestown Heights B3
Kindlestown Lower C3
Kindlestown Park C3
Kindlestown Rise B3
Kinlen Road D3
La Touche Close D2
La Touche Park C2
La Touche Place D2
La Touche Road D2
Lower Grattan Park C2
Manor Avenue D3
Marine Road D2
Marine Terrace D2
Meadow Court C3
Mill Road D3
Mill Road D4
Millbrook D4
Millgrove C4
Millgrove Close C4
Mount Haven D1
Mountain View Park C2
New Road D2
Oakdene B4
Oaklands C2
Oaklands Court C2
Old Mill Road D3
Orchard View D3
Park Lane D3
Pavilion Road D3
Portland Place D3
Portland Road C3
Priory Rise D3
Priory Way C3
Quarry Road D3
Rathdown Close C2
Rathdown Court C2
Rathdown Lawn C2
Rathdown Park C2
Rathdown Road C1
Rathdown Road C2
Redford C1
Redford Court C1
Redford Park C1
Redford Rise C1
Rivendell Grove C3
Riverfield B3
Saint Crispins C1
Saint Vincent Road D3
Salem Vale C4
Sea View C1
Sidmonton Place D2
Somerby Road D3
South Place D3
St. Bridget's Park C2
The Arch D2
The Bawn D2
The Manor D2
The Nurseries C3
The Poplars C3
Trafalgar Court D2
Trafalgar Road D2
Turn Pike Lane D2
Upper Grattan Park C2
Valley View B4
Victoria Road D2
Wendon Brook C4
Whitshed Road D3
Willow Bank C2
Willowmere C1
Woodlands D3

A
B
COOLAGAD
KINDLESTOWN UPPE
GREYSTONES
DELGANY
82
83
84
85
BALLYDONAGH LANE
Kindlestown Rise
Kindlestown Heights
BELLEVUE DEMESNE
To Bray & Dublin
Bellevue Cottages
St Mary's Church (RC)
Bellevue Lawns
Monastery
Oakdene
Convent Court
Church (in Ruins)
Cross
Grave Yd.
Delgany Golf Course
Club House
Valley View
N11
Glen of the Downs
R762
Struan H
Woodland's Church (In Ruins)
Fair Green
DRUMMIN WEST
To Wicklow Town & Arklow
STILEBAWN
BLACKBERRY LANE
2
3
4

Blacklion Manor
Rathdown Park
La Touche Park
New Road
Fairfield Park
Sailing Club
The Bawn
The Arch
Mountain View Park
Victoria Road
Clinic
Sports Ground
Willow Bank
Rathdown Lawn
Saint Killian's RC Church
Rathdown Road
R761
R762
Rathdown Close
The Manor
Saint Patrick's National School
Church Gate
Bayswater Tce
Harbour Court
Trafalgar Road
Cliff Road
Sidmonton Place
St Bridget's Park
Rathdown Court
Saint Kevin's National School
Oaklands Court
St Patrick's Church
Nursing Home
Marine Terrace
Trafalgar Court
Saint Brigid's National School
Church (Presb)
Convent
Presbytery
Marine Road
Saint David's Seconday School
The Grey Stones
Chapel View
Oaklands
Church Lane
Turn Pike Lane
La Touche Close
Kimberley Road
Church Of The Holy Rosary
Parish Hall
Applewood Drive
Church Road
Eden Road
La Touche Road
La Touche Place
Kimberley Court
Presbytery
Applewood Heights
Hillside
Bellevue Park
Hillside Evangelical Church
Chapel Road
Lower Grattan Park
Bellevue Road
Bellevue Park
PO
Greystones Rail Station
Hethervue
Hillside Road
Burnaby Manor
Burnaby Mews
Burnaby Road
Upper Grattan Park
Beechbrook Park
Rivendell Grove
Kindlestown Park
Killincarrick Road
Burnaby Park
Bowling Green
Saint Vincent Road
Mill Road
Kenmare Heights
Bellevue Heights
Pavilion Road
Somerby Road
Park Lane
Saint Laurence's School
Kindlestown Lower
Whitshed Road
South Place
Greystones Golf Course
Portland Road
Portland Place
District Co. Council Office
Club House
Erskine Avenue
The Poplars
Hawkins Lane
Quarry Road
Park
Burnaby Woods
Kinlen Road
Nurseries
Delgany Glen
Burnaby Heights
Old Mill Road
Manor Avenue
Carraig Orchard
Castle (In Ruins)
Castlefield Tce.
Hillcrest Ave
Priory Way
Priory Rise
Cherry Orchard
Castle Villas
Woodlands
Adare Close
Burnaby Park
Greystones Rugby Club
Killincarrig
Orchard View
Carrick Villas
Delgany Wood
Carrig Villas
Delgany National School
Salem Vale
Wendon Brook
Burnaby Mill
Sports Grounds
Greystones Lawn Tennis Club
Delgany Park
Burnaby Avenue
Millgrove
Millbrook
Burnaby Lawns
Millgrove Close
Burnaby Court
Charlesland
Charlesland Court
Charlesland Wood
Fairways
Farrankelly
Glenbrook Park
Area Under Construction
Charlesland Park
To Kilcoole & Wicklow Town
2
3
4

NOTES